PREFACE

This workbook has been created to address the training needs of Managers, Trainers, and Owners of Zip Line and Canopy Tours. This workbook translates current industry standards and best practices into practical techniques and procedures. These techniques and procedures can be used not only to train staff, but also will support the safety management and the operation of the Zip Line/Canopy Tour.

This workbook does not replace formal training and years of practical experience. Instead, this workbook can best be used as a collection of practical guidelines and tasks to effectively train leaders in the Zip Line/Canopy Tour industry.

The Zip Line/Canopy Tour industry has gone through a rapid growth in the last decade. New technology, gear and influential factors are making the industry very dynamic. Be sure to check out our website: **www.AireLibreInternational.com** often for updates and relevant training programs.

CONTENT

Unit 1
The Canopy/Zip Line Adventure Guide

The Adventure Guide (AG) is one of the most vital and visible players on the adventure course. The guide is responsible for safely conducting a high-risk adventure activity, with inexperienced people, while seamlessly managing the risks. Being a guide is a special job for special people. In a high-risk environment, using interpersonal and technical skills, specialized equipment, and ensuring the health and enjoyment of the participants, the adventure guide must be multi-faceted.

1. Adventure Guides must be leaders capable of:

1.1 Take responsibility and be disciplined.

1.2 Educate others to understand the place they visit and involvement with safety management.

1.3 Serve as a host who creates a favorable environment for the visitor.

1.4 Adapt to different environments and standards, follow policies, handle new equipment, regulations, and standards.

1.5 Attend to their clients, educate them and ensure their safety when living high-risk experiences.

1.6 In some courses, a guide has multiple roles such as managing the operation, marketing, sales, equipment management, and sometimes living at the place.

2. What is an Adventure Guide?

The Association for Challenge Course Technology (ACCT) defines the guide as a trained employee to assist, accompany, supervise and provide instructions to participants of the Zip Line/Canopy Tour. The guide is the person responsible for giving a high quality service to the participants, while offering a program of high-risk activities and ensuring their safety.

3. Adventure Guide Responsibilities

The work of the AG is not limited to leading the group of participants through an adventure, rather they are in charge pf the preparation of the Tour. Some of the tasks of the AG include, but are not limited to:

3.2 Prepare equipment

3.3 Inform the client of the risks

3.4 Interpretation of the natural

environment

3.5 Promote low impact practices to ensure the sustainability of the natural environment

3.6 Promote local culture and customs, and motivate participants to consider their own lives in relation to the environment or culture of the place

3.7 Manage risks

3.8 Follow company policies

3.9 Complete Documents

4. Competencies related to the AG

ACCT recommends which competencies that each AG must possess. The work of the AG must be clear and described by the Human Resources staff. Taking into consideration that the activities carried out by the AG are of high-risk, the operator must ensure that the AG works within their limitations and capacities. Next, the basic competencies related to the work of the AG:

4.1 Competencies related to the work of the AG

4.1.1 Understand and follow the mission and vision of the company.

4.1.2 Know and exercise the adventure program as established by the company.

4.1.3 Know and follow the policies and protocols of the company.

4.1.4 Know and be able to speak several languages.

4.1.5 Interpret the environment.

4.1.6 Possess an adequate physical condition that allows him to perform the tasks satisfactorily.

4.1.7 Possess knowledge that is not limited to the Zip Line/Canopy Tour industry, which allows them to develop positive interactions with customers.

4.2 Competencies related to the participant's safety

In the adventure courses, high risk activities are carried out. For that reason, the safety of the participant is a vital importance and must be exercised by the guide at all times, before, during and after the adventure activity. Competencies related to the safety of participants include, but are not limited to:

4.2.1 Possess the competences to communicate correctly to be able to transmit all the necessary safety information and risks.

4.2.2 Know the participation requirements

and know how to apply them to be able to carry out the screening process correctly.

4.2.3 Assess the physical skills of the customer before participating in the tour.

4.2.4 Possess the competences to communicate effectively matters related risk management, as well as the specific safety information through the orientations and the safety talk before the adventure tour.

4.2.5 Possess the competencies to evaluate the performance and maintain a communication of safety and risk management during the adventure tour.

4.2.6 Possess the competencies to effectively supervise the participants when they are doing technical activities in the adventure.

4.2.7 Possess the competencies to handle behaviors, including problems, and conflicts between the participants.

4.2.8 Be able to adapt the tour for any need or situation that arises with the customers.

4.3 Competencies related to the Course Operation

4.3.1 Possess the competences to be able to manage the fun, learning, the different interests of the clients, and above all, the risks of the activity.

4.3.2 Know how to evaluate the atmospheric and natural conditions before and during the tour, be able to make changes, activate a plan, and vacate the course on emergency routes for the safety of customers and employees.

4.3.3 Know how to make an initial inspection in the course and to know in advance that there is no natural or man-made danger that affects the participation of the clients.

4.3.4 Possess the knowledge to inspect Personal Protective Equipment (PPE) and other equipment.

4.3.5 Possess the competences to manage and communicate the risks in each one of the elements. In the case of Canopy Tours, know how to instruct and manage the departure, travel, and landing of participants on all zip lines and platforms.

4.4 Competencies related to emergency management

4.4.1 Have the skills to provide first aid and handle emergency situations.

4.4.2 Know how to activate and follow the emergency plan, and execute technical rescue maneuvers if necessary.

4.5 Competencies related to Equipment management

4.5.1 Know how to handle specialized equipment according to the manufacturer's instructions.

4.5.2 Possess the necessary skills to manage, inspect, maintain, and properly store connectors, helmets, harness, pulleys, or trolley systems, ropes, various types of slings, chest harnesses, descent or ascent devices, belay devices, rescue equipment and any other that is used for the protection of the clients and employees or for the general operation of the course.

4.6 Competencies related with the use of Belay

4.6.1 Possess the skills to select the belay system, install it and handle it correctly.

4.6.2 Know how to install and manage a "Top Rope", as it is a basic technique to climb, descend individuals, and provide safety in the high elements.

4.6.3 Possess the competencies to install and operate each belay system specific to each element.

4.7 Competencies related to technical skills

4.7.1 Possess the skills to make knots and install anchors systems and belay.

4.7.2 Know how to assemble and dismount the trolley system.

4.7.3 Know how to make redundancy systems to anchors.

4.7.4 Know and handle different descent devices, install them, and use them to descend and control the descent of others.

4.7.5 Know how to work on high elements using lifelines and fall arrest safety systems.

4.7.6 Possess the powers to carry out rescues according to the element.

4.7.7 Know the strengths and correct use of each piece of equipment.

4.8 Competencies related to Zip Lines Operation

4.8.1 Possess the skills to operate Zip Lines and respond to the situations that might occur during the experience.

4.8.2 Provide the Safety Talk and Orientation.

4.8.3 Properly install Personal Protective Equipment to customers.

4.8.4 Explain the techniques and processes to use Zip Lines.

4.8.5 Install the Trolley System properly.

4.8.6 Secure the customer on the take-off platform correctly.

4.8.7 Provide instructions on position, orientation, body control, and hand position during travel and how to activate the brakes if necessary.

4.8.8 Provide instructions to customers about how to slow down and control speed.

4.8.9 Teach and put into effect communication systems.

4.8.10 Know and teach how is the landing process in different platforms.

4.8.11 Understand and know how to install, operate and inspect the brake systems for each Element of the Tour.

4.8.12 Know how to assemble and dismount the participant Trolley System.

4.8.13 Know how to proceed in case of an emergency situation.

4.8.14 Know techniques to retrieve equipment from the Zip Lines.

4.9 Competencies related with the use of Rappelling:

4.9.1 Know how to select anchor points, anchor the rope correctly, and know how to install an independent backup/belay system.

4.9.2 Know how to install and manage the participants from the descent station.

4.9.3 Possess the knowledge to descend using rope from different elements.

4.9.4 Possess the skills to instruct the participants correctly, select and install a correct belay system and know how to establish communication and security commands with customers.

4.9.5 Know how to proceed in case of emergency or perform rescue techniques with ropes and know how to install and use rope climbing systems.

5. Universal Skills

There are certain skills that every AG must possess:

5.1 Technical skills

They are competencies that are used in the adventures. Handle the ropes and the associated equipment. Maintain control and safety of the groups during the activities. Skills needed to resolve situations beyond daily and standard processes.

5.2 Security Skills

They are the competencies to carry out the adventure activities in a safe way. Follow the Operation Manual and have a proactive attitude handling the risks. This includes knowledge of first aid, interpreting the weather, responding to accidents, knowledge of how to perform rescues, etc.

5.3 Environmental skills

These are necessary skills to protect the environment. Any activities performed must cause minimal impact. In addition, knowledge to protect, adapt, and educate others about the ecology, flora and fauna of the place.

5.4 Organizational skills

These are the competencies associated with planning, preparing, and executing all processes and experiences of the program. Risk management skills, alternative or contingency plans, orientation of groups, coordination of transportation, food, and other needs to improve the participant's experience.

5.5 Instructor Skills

These are the competencies necessary to teach participants technical skills related to activity, environment and safety.

5.6 Facilitator Skills

Skills necessary to motivate individual and collective development. Motivate participants to perform tasks while supporting interpersonal relationships and individual needs. This includes skills for conflict resolution, facilitating effective communication, supporting trust, and ensuring group cooperation.

5.7 Flexible Leadership Style

It means knowing how to use different styles of leadership. Sometimes, the AG can make decisions democratically about what activity to do, or which route to choose. During emergencies the AG must be autocratic, give precise directions, and leave behind the group's contribution.

5.8 Experience-based judgment

Good judgment essential because the AG may face new situations with lack of experience. Considering past experiences and using judgment, the AG can make critical decisions. It is of vital importance that the AG use their experiences when making decisions that can affect the health and safety of the participants.

5.9 Problem solving Skills

These are competencies associated with how the AG solves the problems. Solving problems must be a combination of creativity and analysis. Recognizing and identifying problems or situations, defining difficulties, anticipating situations, identifying possible solutions, putting solutions into action and evaluating their effectiveness are some of the necessary skills.

5.10 Decision-Making skills

These are competencies that lead the AG to make the best decisions. The AG should be able to devise and evaluate a variety of options to help make the right decisions, taking in consideration the standards of the Adventure program.

5.11 Effective communication

The AG should be able to communicate effectively, not just with the participants, but with co-workers. Presenting the situation in different ways, clarifying concepts, and providing feedback and other measures.

5.12 Professional Ethics

It refers to the moral standards and values of the AG. Respect, attention, and sensitivity in crisis cases are some of the necessary skills. In addition, the AG have a lot of influence on the participants, it is important not to abuse the power exerting a negative influence on them.

The Essential Functions of a Certified Challenge Course Practitioner by ACCT

1   Range of motion and flexibility

1.1 Perform various positions and postures necessary to conduct practitioner task.

1.2 Manipulate ropes, cables, and other related equipment used in tying knots, belaying, and rigging used in the setup, operation, a breakdown of various challenge course-related systems.

1.3 Physically negotiate various terrain types and/or obstacles confronted during both routine program delivery and emergency situations.

2   Manual Dexterity and Motor Skills

2.1 Operate/utilize various challenge course-related gear and Equipment including, and not limited to, ropes, harness, helmets, carabineers, safety lines, ladders, and pulleys.

2.2 Ascend to, traverse at, and descend from heights that height that may exceed 25 feet (7.62m).

2.3 Relocate, ascend, and descend ladders and various other course access equipment including, and not limited to, cargo nets, stairs, climbing staples, and vertical cables.

3 **Endurance and Stamina**

   3.1 Possess ability and endurance to achieve certification for and carry out site-specific first aid procedures and/or protocols, which may include first aid and Cardio Pulmonary Resuscitation (CPR).

   3.2 Perform required duties for extended periods of time while exposed to adverse conditions including precipitation, temperature extremes, and wind.

4 **Sight and Visual Acuity**

   4.1 Possess good corrected or uncorrected vision.

   4.2 Possess to adequate depth perception to recognize safety hazards in a variety of normal and/or emergency environments.

   4.3 Possess the ability to see, read, and recognize safety hazards in variety of normal and/or emergency environments.

5 **Communication Skills**

   5.1 Communicate in a clear and understandable fashion with participants and other staff members.

   5.2 Able to effectively communicate in an appropriate manner in the programming environment with or without accommodation.

   5.3 Effectively communicate with participants based on their personality type, especially during sensitive, interpersonal contacts.

6 **Reasoning and Decision-making Ability**

   6.1 Comprehend and implement oral and writing instructions.

   6.2 Apply reasoning skills when confronted with circumstances requiring a discretionary decision.

   6.3 Establish priorities and construct further plans after an initial assessment.

   6.4 Formulate and implement an appropriate course of action in each situation for which no specific rule or procedure has been established.

   6.5 Apply theory-based instructions or training to actual incidents/situations.

Unit 2
Understanding the Course

There are some physical components and phenomena that all adventure guides (AG) must know. These aspects of basic physics dictate the behavior of the forces, the angles, and the resistance of the equipment. This information should be translated into knowledge and behaviors that the guide should apply when working on the adventure course.

1. Loads

Two types of loads are experienced in the course during normal operation:

1.1 **Dead Load (static)** – refer to loads that typically don't change over time, such as the weights of materials and components of the structure itself. For example, wire cables and the platform materials.

1.2 **Live Loads (dynamics)** – refer to loads that do, or can, change over time, such as people crossing a bridge or traversing a zip line, including loads that are created naturally by the environment such as wind, snow, seismic, and lateral soil pressures.

1.3 **Shock loading** – refers to a sudden and drastic increase of load, for example, when somebody falls. This situation can damage equipment.

2. Forces & Angle

To know how force and angles manifest, it is necessary to understand Newton's second law. Newton's second law of motion pertains to the behavior of objects for which all existing forces that are not balanced. The second law states that the acceleration of an object is dependent upon two variables, the force acting upon the object and the mass of the object.

3. Application

Newton's second law is expressed when a force is applied to an angle. For example, when a weight (the participant) exerts force on a line (lifeline or Zip Line cable) an angle is formed. This angle as shown in the next image, can be dynamic when the weight is moving or static, or when the weight has stopped moving.

When there is a weight (participant) exerting force (weight) on a line, the resulting angle among other factors, combine to transmit an amplified force through the vectors (lifelines) to the anchor points. According to the weight and the angle, it will be the resulting force at the anchor points.

4. Load

In order to measure the load or force that results from the weight (the participant) and is directed to the anchors, the formula is:

$F = ma$

F = is the force

m = is the mass or participant weight

a = is the attraction of the gravity force

The result of this formula expressed in Newton (N), which is used to know the resulting force to the anchors. In other words, this measure represents the applied force. Then, one (1) N is the amount of force that is needed to move 1kg of mass at a rate of one (1) meter per square second. This is a relatively small unit, for that reason, in the field it is expressed in kN (1,000 N). It is important to know that a Newton is a measure that belongs to the International System of Unit (SI). In the United States it is also expressed in pounds (lbf).

In the next image it can be seen as the angle grows, the strength increases in the components especially at the anchor point. Is important to note that at 120 degrees the initial weight is doubled, doubling the load on each of the anchor points including the components.

Resultant Forces

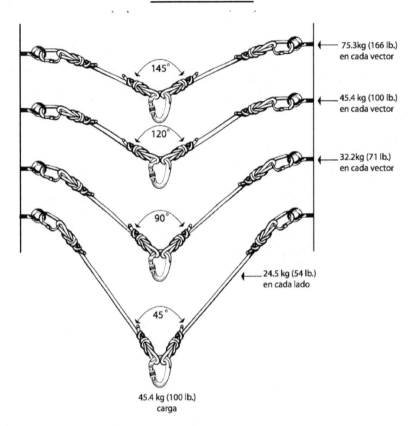

75.3kg (166 lb.)
en cada vector

145°

45.4 kg (100 lb.)
en cada vector

120°

32.2kg (71 lb.)
en cada vector

90°

24.5 kg (54 lb.)
en cada lado

45°

45.4 kg (100 lb.)
carga

5. Application in the Zip Lines

This situation where the forces multiply through the vectors because of the weight has a special connotation for the Zip Line. This is because a static weight, let's say a customer standing in the middle of the cable, can form angles of up to 145 degrees or more. That means the customer's weight will more than double. It is also important to know that a participant can generate a vertical load of 2.2 KN (500 lbs).

Of course, all that force is distributed along the Zip Line (vectors) to the anchors. Builders must design zip lines with a deflection of at least 5% so that the tension is maintained below 10.2 KN (2.304 lbs) in traditional 3/8 inches wire cable.

In other words, keep the tension below 2.304 lbs (10.2 kN), in case of using steel wire with a diameter of 3/8 ". Being 2.304 lb. The Working Loads Limits (WLL) of a 3/8 "steel cable" with terminations. To know which is the WLL of a steel cable, you can run the following calculation:

14

WLL of a 3/8" belay (lifeline) wire rope Cable

- The 3/8" wire rope cable has a breaking strength rated at 14,400 lbs. (6540kg)

- According to the manufacturer U or J style clips termination have a rated reduction of 20% (.20) on cables.

- Then, 14,400 x .20 = 2,880 lbs. (1308 kg) WLL of Cable

- Formula: <u>WLL of cable</u> X <u>strength of cable after clip reduction</u> = WLL of cable with termination.

- E.g. 2,880 (3/8" wire cable WLL) multiplicated by .80 (80% of strength after cables clip reduction) = 2,304 lb. (WLL of cable with termination).

6. Fall factor

The fall factor is a term used to describe the relationship between the fall distance of a person and the length of rope available to arrest or stop the fall. The fall factor is calculated as follows:

Fall Factor = Fall distance / Length available to arrest the fall.

The measurements are considered from the anchorage point to the connection point in the user's harness.

6.1 <u>Fall Factor 0</u>

The person is connected to a higher anchor point with a rope or lifeline not greater than 6 feet (1.82 m). To be connected directly to a higher anchorage point, there is no chance of falling

6.2 <u>Fall Factor 1</u>

A person connected with a lifeline or rope approximately, at the level of the connection point of the harness. If this person falls, the fall distance will be equal to half of the rope available to arrest its fall.

6.3 <u>Fall Factor 2</u>

In this case, the lifeline of the person is anchored to the level of their feet. In this situation, if a fall occurs, the rope would have to completely stretch its distance in order to arrest the fall. In other words, the fall will theoretically be the length of the available rope.

This situation brings an implication for the adventure guide. The safest and least likely way to cause damage is with a fall factor 0. If you have to connect fall factor 1 or 2, it is important to consider the type of lanyards, harness and fall arrest system.

7. The Strength of the Equipment

The Equipment used in Zip Line/Canopy Tours are not indestructible. For that reason, manufacturers of reliable and certified equipment perform tests to determine in effect, what is the strength of them.

In general, the strength of the equipment is expressed in two ways:

    7.1 Breaking strength

    7.2 Working load limit

7.1 Breaking Strength

Breaking strength also known as Ultimate Strength refers to the load in which the material or assembly of materials fail to support the applied load. That is, with the load that the piece of Equipment breaks or permanently deforms.

The breaking strength calculation, is a measurement of the average force at which the product, under the conditions it would leave the factory, has been broken by a constantly increasing force applied in a direct line to the product at a uniform speed in a standard tensile test machine.

In general, the Personal Protective Equipment (PPE) used in the operation of the Zip Line/Canopy Tour is identified with Breaking Strength. In practice, in Adventure Courses the Breaking Strength of the Life Safety Systems is 5,000 lbf or 22.2 kN.

ACCT defines Life Safety Systems as a configuration of components including lifelines, belay beams, and anchorage that support fall restraint and arrest systems, personal safety systems, belay systems, and/or rope rigging systems.

Breaking Strengths can also be expressed in Average Breaking Strength (ABS) which determines the averaging of samples in a given test and Minimum Breaking Strength (MBS) which is determined in several ways among them using the true minimum number that was recorded during a testing sample or more commonly by using a statistical method such as 3-Sigma. In the Zip Line / Canopy Tours industry, Minimum Breaking Strength is considered equivalent to Breaking Strengths

7.2 Working Load Limits

Working Load Limit (WLL), Safe Working Limit (SWL) or Maximum Rated Load (MRL) is the maximum allowable load on a component or system during normal service as determined by the designer or manufacturer. In other words, is the maximum load which should ever be applied to the product.

Typically, the rigging Equipment is marked with WLL.

In general, the manufacturer calculates using the following formulas:

- **Safety factor**= Breaking strength/WLL
- **WLL** = Breaking Strength / Safety factor.

For service or design purposes, use the Working Load Limit instead of Breaking Strength. Breaking Strengths, when published, were obtained under controlled laboratory conditions. The list of breaking strength does not mean that the working load limit should ever be exceeded.

8. Fall Protection

A reliable solution that protects employees from falls when they are working in high risk environment 6 feet or more but doesn't interfere with the work being performed. There is no universal solution for fall protection and the best system will depend on a number of different factors such as job task and space constraints.

Fall Protection Systems must be connected to an anchor point. In the Zip Line Canopy/Tour rather, in each element there must be an anchor point approved or manufactured to be used by the adventure guide. This anchor point must have a Braking Strength of at least 5,000 lbf or 22.2 kN. In general terms in the Zip Line/Canopy Tours the following are used as an anchor points:

8.1 Zip Lines cables

8.2 Zip Line Anchors with Eye Bolts

8.3 Zip Line Anchors with yokes

8.4 Element Belay cables

8.5 Belay hoops

8.6 Breaking Systems

8.7 Rappelling Anchor Systems

8.8 Vertical Fall Arrest Systems.

9. Fall Protection Systems

There is a variety of fall protection systems. In Canopy/Zip Line Tours generally use 2 types of systems when the guides are working at more than 6 feet in height:

9.1 Personal Fall Arrest Systems

9.2 Fall Restraint Systems

9.1 Personal Fall Arrest Systems

A personal fall arrest system is a system used to safely arrest (stop) a worker falling from heights.

It consists of connectors, a body harness, lanyard, energy absorbers, lifeline, or a combination of these. The operator and the type of elements will dictate if this type of fall arrest system is required for operate the element.

9.1.1 Energy Absorber

Energy Absorbers are used where there is the probability of falling from above. In that case, the end of the lanyard has to be connected to an energy absorber.

The energy absorber consists of a tubular tape sewn in a zigzag or "Z" shape wrapped in a container or package that, in the event of a fall, these seams break creating the effect of cushioning the impact of the blow. Fall Arrest Systems must have a minimum strength of 5,000 lbs. (22.2 kN).

9.2 Fall Restraint Systems

In the basic restriction system, the participant or guide will never be able to approach the border because the system restricts it. The Guide is connected directly from his harness to an anchor point. In this case, no fall arrest system is used because when restricted, the possibility of a fall null.

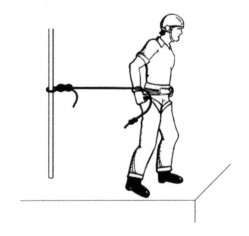

Unit 3
Equipment & Inspection

PPE Description

Personal Protective Equipment (PPE) is an umbrella name that is used to specifically group the Equipment that protects the Adventure Guide and the participant from falling from heights. The PPE must be of high quality, reliable, validated and certified and consists of a harness, helmets, carabiner, pulleys, lifelines, and ropes. It is of the utmost importance that they are handled, maintained, stored and inspected properly.

Strength

The international strength standard for safety Equipment is 5.000 lbs. (22.2 KN). In this way and with devices with this minimum strength as standard, the life safety equipment is covered with a safety factor 10:1 either in a static or dynamic system.

Harness

The purpose of the harness is to tie and hold the body (weight) of the user to an anchor point, rope, a descent device, a Trolley system, lifeline, or a fall arrest system when an individual is at high altitudes or in a high risk place, where there is the possibility of falling.

1. Characteristics of a Good Harness

In general, a harness should:

  1.1 Have a good center of gravity

  1.2 Be strong and safe

  1.3 Have an accessible anchor point.

  1.4 Have space to carry additional equipment.

  1.5 Have redundancy for the harness to remain secure in case the connection point fails.

  1.6 Be certified by relevant agencies.

  1.7 Be comfortable, light and with the ability to adjust to the body, difference clothing and changing the size of the user.

  1.8 Be able to absorb energy in case of a fall.

2. Types of Harness

Harnesses are manufactured as follows:

2.1 Waist Harness

This is the type of basic harness that supports the user's waist and legs.

2.2 Full Body Harness

It is a type of waist harness to which a chest harness is added, so it provides back and body support in general.

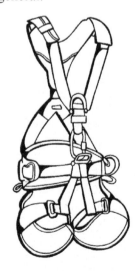

2.3 Chest Harness

The chest harness straps and holds the upper body, but cannot be used alone, i.e. without a waist harness. This type of harness takes a special function on the Zip Line as it is used to keep the user upright or in a certain position, preventing the upper part of the body from falling by the effect of gravity.

3. Harness Syndrome

When a individual hangs from the harness without movement, the straps tighten or create a kind of tourniquet on the legs by pressing the arteries and obstructing the blood circulation and causing heart problems. The consequence is extreme pain, blood accumulation in the legs and changes in blood pressure. This situation creates a possible fatal condition that increases the more time passes.

The biggest recommendation is to provide immediate help to any individual who is hanging without movement in his harness.

4. Certifications

Harnesses must comply with one of the following certifications:

United State Certifications

ANSI Z359

NFPA 1983

ASTM 1772

Europe Certifications

UIAA 105

EN 12277

Helmets

Outdoor activities are high-risk and may pose serious hazards to the head, especially with objects falling from a height. For that reason, the helmet is an integral part of the PPE. The helmet not only protects the user from falling objects height, but strikes against obstacles and objects (steel cables, platforms, stairs, poles, trees, etc.).

1. Characteristics of a Good Helmet

A helmet must have the following characteristics:

1.1 The suspension system should be able to absorb the impact energy so that it is not transmitted to the head, neck, or spine.

1.2 The shell design must protect the user from objects falling from heights and from side blows.

1.3 It must be adjusted correctly so that it does not interrupt the vision.

1.4 It must have a thin ridge at the front to prevent water droplets from falling on the user's face.

1.5 It should be light, provide ventilation and allow you to listen.

1.6 If the helmet does not provide information, the operator must contact the manufacturer to learn about the certifications and recommendations for use, inspection and maintenance.

1.7 The chinstrap must have an easy-to-disconnect buckle system.

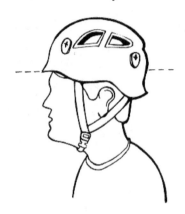

2. Certifications

Helmets must comply with one of the following certifications:

<u>European Certifications</u>

UIAA 106

EN 12492

<u>United States Certifications</u>

ANSI Z89.1

NFPA 1951

CSA 294.1

Carabiner

The carabiner is a piece of Equipment made of aluminum, steel and other materials that has a gate with springs that allows to connect the ropes, descent devices, trolley systems, lanyards, anchor systems, and rescue systems. Its function in connect all parts of metal and textile Equipment

1. Strengths

Industry practices require that all carabiners used to connect lives have a breaking point of at least 5.000 lbs. (22.2 KN)

2. Shape and Design

Carabiners are manufactured in a variety of shapes, sizes, materials and styles of operation. In general, there are 3 designs:

2.1 Oval shape

2.2 D shape

2.3 Pear shape

2.1 Oval shape

The carabiner in Oval is the weakest because of its shape, distributes the weight equally. For that reason, the weight goes equally to the gate which is the weaker part of this piece of Equipment. Even so, some manufacturers design pieces of Equipment for this type of carabiner.

2.2 D shape

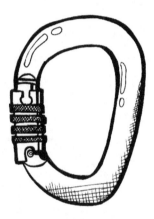

Carabiners are manufactured in the form of a "D" for a simple reason, to get the weight away from the gate, which is the weakest part, placing in the major axis of the connector, which is the strongest part.

2.3 Pear shape (HMS)

The pear-shaped carabiners, also known as HMS by the German word "Halbmastwurfsicherung", provide more space. The gate is more open and designed to be used with the Munter Hitch knot.

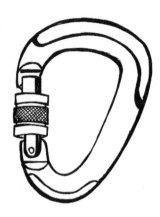

3. Wrong position

If a carabiner turns by mistake or oversight and receives weight on the gate, it may fail. The strength of the carabiner can be reduced by 10 KN if force is applied to the gate and could break with only a force of 500 to 2.500 lbs. (227 to 1.134 kg).

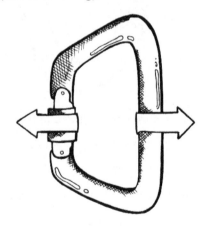

4. Lock

Basically, carabiners are manufactured with two types of locks: threaded and automatic:

4.1 Screw Lock

This type has a kind of thread and nut on the gate. To close it, screw the lock in direction to the nose of the carabiner.

4.2 Automatic Lock

This type of lock has a spring which, when opened, is closed and locked automatically.

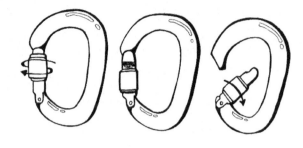

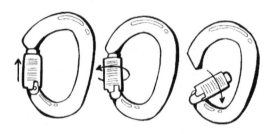

5. Certifications

Carabiners must comply with one of the following certifications:

European Certifications

EN 12275

EN 362

UIAA 121

United States Certifications

CSA Z259

ANSI Z359

NFPA 1983 (2012). This test has the categories Escape (E), Technical (T) and General (G) to classify carabiners and other pieces of equipment. Each one of these has different properties. "Escape" is associated with personal equipment, "technical" is associated with technical and general applications (G) to rescue situations in general. For that reason, it is important that the adventure guide and the operator know what type of carabiner is right for the work they intend to do.

Pulleys

A pulley is a device that rotates freely on metal wheels, used to reduce the friction on the ropes/cables, and has a side plates where the carabiner is connected.

There is a wide variety of pulleys, each manufactured with different purposes, for example:

    a.   Rescue situations.

    b.   Mechanical Advantage Systems.

    c.   Changes direction of ropes.

    d.   To pass knots.

    e.   Trolley Systems.

1. Type of Pulley used in Zip Lines

There is a wide variety of pulleys that are used as Trolley. The distances and sizes of the lifelines among other factors, will dictate what type of pulleys to use.

In traditional Zip Line/Canopy Tours where lifelines with diameter between 3/8" and 1/2" are used, the type of pulley used is with two wheels (sheaves) in lines, manufactured in stainless steel with fixed side plate. The side plates of this type of pulley are fixed, unlike the traditional pulleys whose side plates rotate to be installed.

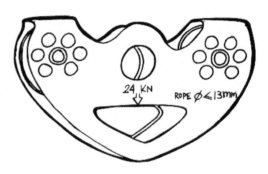

This type of trolley accepts up to three carabiners at the lower connection point, which is the main one. In the upper part there is another connection point with space for a carabiner. The purpose of this upper connection point is to connect the Trolleys to other, for double lifeline systems.

2. Trolley Installation

The following steps explain how to properly install the pulley:

    2.1 Slide the pulley on the side of the anchor point and insert the steel wire or rope into it.

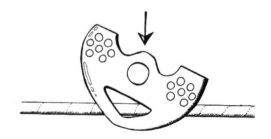

2.2 Once the cable or rope is inside the pulley, place a carabiner at the anchor point.

2.3 The carabiner serves as a connection point for the Trolley lanyard.

3. Strength requirements of pulleys used as Trolley

The ACCT standard recommends that pulleys used in Trolley systems for being part of the PPE require a minimum strength of 5.000 lbs (22.2 KN).

4. Certifications

Pulleys must comply with any of the following certifications:

European Certifications

UIAA 127
EN 12278

United States Certifications

NFPA 1983

Lanyards

A lanyard is a short piece of rope, webbing or steel cable whose purpose is to connect the user with the components of the course or an anchor point. There are four types of lanyards: adjustable, mechanically adjustable, with steel cables and fixed lines. Customers and Adventure Guides (AG) must use lanyards to prevent a fall from heights. These places could be Zip Lines, aerial bridges, crossings of high horizontal elements, and aerial platforms.

1. What kind of lanyard use?

The fall factor and the type of fall protection required are largely dictated by the type of lanyard to be used. For example:

1.1 Fall Factor = 0

Recommendation: static ropes

1.2 Fall Factor less than 1 (between 0 and 1)

Recommendation: Semi-static ropes

1.3 Fall Factor greater than 1 (between 1 and 2)

Recommendation: Dynamic ropes with full body harness.

1.4 Fall Factor 2

Recommendation: Dynamic ropes with full body harness.

2. Simple lanyards

They provide a connection between the user's harness and an anchor point.

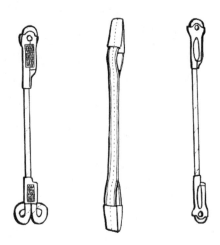

3. Double Lanyards

Double lanyards are used in situations where the user must transfer from one element to another. At the time of transfer, you can disconnect one of the lines and connect it to the new element and then transfer the second line. That way, you can pass over obstacles or simply switch items without being disconnected. This type of lanyard is also known as Lobster Claws.

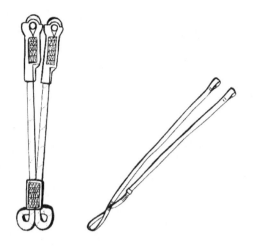

4. Smart Double Lanyards

The technology of the "Smart Belay" of the company Edelrid provides a system in which when a carabiner of a lanyard is open, for example, to transfer from one element to another, the second carabiner will be closed, and it will not be open by the participant until he connects the one they have in their hand. If one of the carabiners is disconnected, the other must be closed and so on. That way, the participant will never be devoid of security since one of the two lines will always be connected.

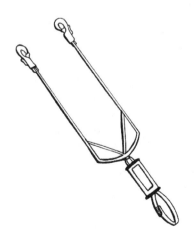

5. Asymmetrical Lanyards

This type of lanyards is used to progress through high-risk locations and transfer from one connection point to another. It is also used to assemble the Trolley system as it Is having a short and a long side, it allows the easy connection of the pulleys to the system of double steel wire.

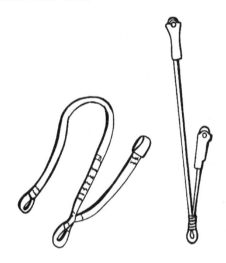

6. During the progression of the Canopy/Zip Line Tour, the lanyard should be used for the following purposes:

6.1 Transfers from zip lines to elements and vice versa.

6.2 Transfers from zip lines to aerial bridges and vice versa.

6.3 Zip line transfers to zip lines.

6.4 On the take-off and arrival platforms.

6.5 In the Trolley Systems.

6.6 On aerial bridges.

6.7 In high elements.

6.8 In jump stations.

6.9 In pendulum stations.

6.10 In the Adventure Towers.

6.11 On rappelling stations.

7. Strengths Requirements

The ACCT recommends that personal lanyards must have a minimum strength of 5.000 lbs. (22.2 KN).

8. Certifications

Lanyards must comply with one of the following certifications:

<u>European Certifications</u>

EN 354

EN 795B

Ropes

The ropes as well as other pieces of equipment are essential for the operation of the Adventure Course. With ropes the people can ascend and descend from heights, use them to protection in high risk places and rescue others that need help.

1. Types of synthetic fibers

The ropes are manufactured with various materials. Traditionally they are made with nylon, polyester and with high modulus polyethylene fibers such as Spectra & Dyneema

General Features

1.1 Nylon

1.1.1 Stretches from 15% to 28% to its breaking point

1.1.2 Abrasion resistance

1.1.3 Loses strength when getting wet.

1.1.4 Weak in the face of ultraviolet rays and metal contacts

1.1.5 Weak to concentrates of acids, especially the contents in the batteries and other chemicals like hydrogen peroxide, phenols, Cresol and Xyleneles

1.1.6 Weak before whitening agents

1.1.7 Energy absorption

1.2 Polyester

Strength and durability

1.2.1 Resistance to acid damage

1.2.2 Does not float

1.2.3 Susceptible to strong alkali damage

1.2.4 Resistance to ultraviolet rays

1.2.5 Little Stretch

1.2.6 Low resistance to falls

1.2.7 Abrasion-resistant

1.2.8 Hydrophobic

1.2.9 Weak versus strong alkaline and ammonium

1.3 Spectra & Dyneema

1.3.1 Stretches well

1.3.2 10 times stronger than steel

1.3.3 Stretches from 2.7% to 3.5% before breaking point

1.3.4 Resists certain acids and chemicals

1.3.5 Resistant to cuts and abrasions

1.3.6 Little skill for knots

1.3.7 UV-Resistant

1.3.8 Little ability to absorb energy from fall.

2. Types of constructions

Throughout history, the ropes have been built in several ways. Currently, the type of rope construction used in Adventure Courses is known as Kernmantle.

2.1 Kernmantle

The German term "Kernmantle" means strong fibers in the center (Kern), covered by an external braiding (mantle) surrounding the internal fibers. This type of rope, since its creation, has dominated adventure sports and rescues.

The purpose of the cover or mantle is to protect the internal fibers from damage from dust, sun, and abrasions, among others. The internal fibers resist from 70% to 90% of the total strength of the rope. The internal fibers and their cover create a relationship that determines the characteristics or properties of the rope.

The properties can be:

    2.1.1 Elasticity
    2.1.2 Grip on the user's hand
    2.1.3 Ability to make knots
    2.1.4 Flexibility
    2.1.5 Strengths
    2.1.6 Temperature resistance
    2.1.7 Ability to absorb impacts
    2.1.8 Lifetime
    2.1.9 Sliding of the cover.

2.2 Static Kernmantle

The static ropes traditionally are built with a center composed of uniform, linear, and parallel nylon fibers, which are covered by an outer braided polyester or nylon. Its maximum stretch is 6% to 10%, to 10% of its minimum rupture force.

Because this type of rope has no elasticity properties, it is used for tasks like rope descents, rescues and to descend and ascend large weights. Static ropes are not good at absorbing fall impacts, unlike dynamic ropes.

2.3 Semi-Static Kernmantle

This is a type of static rope that has a little more elasticity properties because it has few kinks in the internal fibers. The difference between semi-static and static is relatively little. The semi-static rope stretches between 6% and 10%, to 10% of its minimum rupture force. When in use, it stretches between 1% to 5% with body weight.

These properties of elasticity do not make it a dynamic rope because it is not good at absorbing energy, but, they are highly abrasion-resistant ropes, the internal part supports 100% of the weight, allowing the external part not to lose strength when it suffers abrasions.

2.4 Dynamic Kernmantle

The dynamic ropes possess the property of arresting or stopping the free fall of an individual in a mountaineering situation with a limited impact force. The dynamic term refers to the ability to absorb falls, as people who fall from heights. This type of rope sacrifices resistance to abrasions and strength to reach the property of absorbing energy.

The construction of this type of rope is based on fibers being twisted in different directions, covered by a braid of polyester or nylon.

3. Some of the care the AG should have with the Ropes are:

3.1 Avoid contact of the rope with acids, chemicals, and other abrasive liquids.

3.2 Avoid exposing the rope to car fumes.

3.3 Do not place it on the concrete floor as it is alkaline and contains substances that affect the fiber of the rope.

3.4 Do not store in humid locations

3.5 Do not store in high-temperature places.

4. Basic technique for storing the rope in a rope bag

The simplest and recommended method that an AG could use to store the rope in the Rope Bag is as follows:

4.1 Open the package, place it in a position where it is easy to enter the rope.

4.2 Take the tip of the rope and take it to the bottom.

4.3 With the tip of the rope at the bottom of the bag, take another piece of rope and slide into the bottom of the bag.

4.4 Repeat the step, take more rope and insert it to the bottom of the bag, but keep in mind that every new rope you put in the bag, must be above the rope that was already inside.

4.5 Each time you enter more rope, make sure to accommodate it above the previous one.

4.6 This way, when you remove the rope from the bag, it will come out in sequence from the top to the bottom of the bag, thus avoiding tangling with itself.

Coiling the Rope

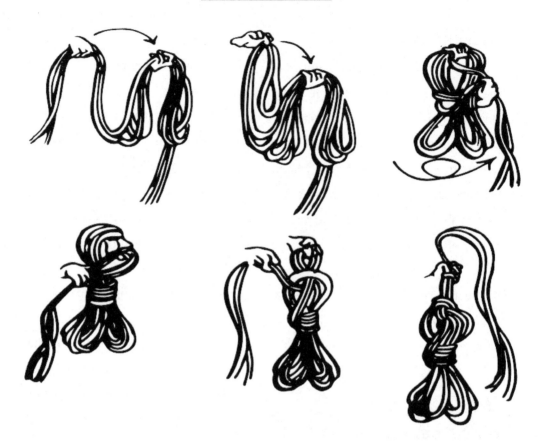

5. Certifications

The ropes must comply with one of the following certifications:

Dynamic Ropes

European Certifications

UIAA 101

EN 892

Static and Semi-static ropes

European Certifications

UIAA 107

EN 1891 (Tipo A)

United States Certifications

NFPA 1983

CI 1801

Equipment Inspection

Personal Protective Equipment (PPE) is a series of equipment utilized to protect individuals from falling in a high-risk environment. This equipment generally is made with metals, textiles, and plastic. The next list provides inspection criteria for metals and textile. For plastic pieces use textiles criteria.

1. How to Inspect Equipment

It is the responsibility and task of the AG to inspect its PPE each time it is used, as well as to inspect the equipment used with the participants every day.

It is important to highlight the fact that the AG is not a professional inspector. Therefore, is expected to know at least the basic inspection criteria to evaluate the condition of the equipment used daily.

The PPE can be damaged for several reasons in a short period of time. For that reason, the basic inspection of the PPE must be done daily. It is unacceptable and a bad practice of risk management to use PPE that at least have not received a basic inspection. The PPE may be affected and that can translate into an emergency situation.

This situation puts in the AG a daily responsibility, inspect the PPE in a basic way, before carrying out the adventure tour. It is the responsibility of the Guide to ensure that all participants are properly protected when they are in high risk environments.

2. How to Perform the Inspection

Before inspecting the PPE, the Guide must know the inspection criteria are. In other words, he would have to know what you are going to inspect on each piece of Equipment in particular. The tools to perform the inspection are two, Visual and Tactile:

2.1 Visual Inspection

This way of inspecting requires that the guide observes the parts and components of equipment, each one with its different criteria.

If the guide has any questions, he can compare the piece of equipment with others, to know if it has all its parts and components. If the guide have a question beyond that, the recommendation is not to use the Equipment, document it and send it to the local or professionals of the course.

2.2 Tactile Inspection

This way of inspecting requires that the guide touch with their hands and feel the condition of the materials. For that, the guide must know the inspection criteria for each piece of equipment.

When touching the pieces of equipment, the guide must decide by touch if the parts or component have been modified or if they are in perfect condition. If the guide has any doubt about the operation of the piece of equipment, he can test its operation to know it is working properly. If the guide has a question beyond that, the recommendation is to not use the piece of equipment. Instead document it and send it to the local or professionals of the course.

3. Materials Inspection Criteria

When inspecting the equipment tactilely and visually, the AG must seek and evaluate the following inspection criteria. Excessive expression of one or more of these criteria, it is a reason to not use it. In that case, document it and send it to the course inspectors.

3.1 Metal Criteria:

3.1.1 Excessive wear

3.1.2 Deformation

3.1.3 Deflections

3.1.4 Cracks

3.1.5 Grooves

3.1.6 Marks

3.1.7 Rust, corrosion, and oxidation

3.1.8 Burrs

3.2 Textile Criteria:

3.2.1 Excessive wear

3.2.2 Deformation

3.2.3 Burns

3.2.4 Chemical damage

3.2.5 Stains

3.2.6 Marks

3.2.7 Cuts

3.2.8 Frays

3.2.9 Cuts

3.2.10 Torn

3.2.11 Threads pulled or cuts

3.2.12 Soft or stiff spots

3.2.13 Cut or torn stitched

3.2.14 Glazing

4. Specific Equipment Criteria

The following are the specific inspection criteria for the equipment:

4.1 Belay Devices

4.1.1 Condition of the fixed and moving side parts.

4.1.2 Condition of the friction components.

4.1.3 Condition of the handle.

4.1.4 Condition of the locking components.

4.1.5 Effectiveness of the return spring of the cam.

4.1.6 Effectiveness of the return spring of the handle.

4.1.7 Ease of opening and closing of the moving side parts.

4.1.8 Operational test on the rope.

4.2 Descender

4.2.1 Condition of the fixed and moving side parts.

4.2.2 Condition of the friction components.

4.2.3 Condition of the of the locking components.

4.2.4 Condition of the anti-panic catch stop.

4.2.5 Effectiveness of the return springs of the cam, safety catch, and anti-panic catch.

4.2.6 Ease of opening and closing of the moving side parts.

4.2.7 Verify that the moving side-parts cannot be closed without properly engaging the cam axle.

4.2.8 Operational test on the rope.

4.3 Connectors

4.3.1 Condition of the body of the connector.

4.3.2 Condition of the hook or nose of the connector.

4.3.3 Condition of the gate of the connector, rivet and of the locking sleeve.

4.3.4 Check of the correct functioning of the gate.

4.3.5 Correct alignment of the gate and the hook.

4.3.6 Effectiveness of the return spring and articulation of the gate.

4.3.7 Operation of the locking system.

4.4 Harness

4.4.1 Condition of the webbing.

4.4.2 Condition of the load-bearing stitching.

4.4.3 Condition of the connection points.

4.4.4 Condition of the adjustment buckles.

4.4.5 Condition and compatibility of the connector.

4.4.6 Condition of protective components.

4.4.7 Condition of padding of the waist belt and leg-loop, jacket part, back support, and gear loop straps.

4.4.8 Condition of the non-load-bearing stitching.

4.4.9 Operational test.

4.5 Helmets

4.5.1 Condition of the exterior of the shell.

4.5.2 Condition of the interior of the shell.

4.5.3 Condition of the cradle headband, webbing, stitching, molded parts, fastening buckles.

4.5.4 Condition of the fixing components of the cradle/headband.

4.5.5 Condition of the padding of the headband.

4.5.6 Condition of the clips for headlamp mounting

4.5.7 Operation of the headband adjustment.

4.5.8 Operation of the nape strap adjustment.

4.5.9 Operation of the forward/rearward adjustment of the chin strap.

4.5.10 Operation of the opening, closing and the adjustment of the chin strap.

4.6 Lanyards

4.6.1 Condition of the rope or webbing.

4.6.2 Condition of stitching.

4.6.3 Condition of the friction components.

4.6.4 Condition of the locking components.

4.6.5 Free rotation of the moving parts.

4.6.6 Condition of the comfort components.

4.6.7 Compatibility of the lanyard with the metallic parts.

4.6.8 Compatibility with the connectors.

4.6.9 Condition of the connectors.

4.6.10 Check of the lanyard's length. adjustment system.

4.6.11 Check of function of connector.

4.7 Ropes

4.7.1 Condition of the sheath.

4.7.2 Tactile check of the core.

4.7.3 Condition of the stitching at sewn terminations.

4.7.4 Condition of knots.

4.7.5 Check of the length.

4.7.6 Condition of the protective components.

4.8 Pulleys

4.8.1 Condition of the body.

4.8.2 Condition of the moving side parts.

4.8.3 Condition of the connection holes.

4.8.4 Condition of the grooves of the sheaves.

4.8.5 Condition of the axle.

4.8.6 Condition of the cam.

4.8.7 The sheave turns freely.

4.8.8 Check of the opening and closing of the side parts.

4.8.9 Function of the cam return spring.

4.8.10 Function of the safety catch.

5. Maintenance

5.1 General recommendations

5.1.1 Don't leave the equipment on the floor.

5.1.2 Read and apply the manufacturer's use, care, maintenance and storage recommendations.

5.1.3 Know the lifetime of your equipment (e.g., PETZL, 10 years in textile and plastic products).

5.1.4 Keep the Equipment in packages.

5.1.5 Don't leave equipment in places with extreme temperatures.

5.1.6 Keep the equipment in ventilated places, no sun rays (UV).

5.1.7 Store away from chemicals and acids.

5.1.8 No stores in humid places or flooded with water, can grow mold and other conditions.

5.1.9 In places with a lot of salt, protect it rinsing with fresh water.

5.2 Metal Equipment

5.2.1 Rinse the metal equipment with fresh, clean water after use in salty places or near the sea.

5.2.2 Use a small brush, if necessary, to remove dirt or corrosion from the equipment part.

5.2.3 Use warm water and neutral soap (PH neutral) to wash metal equipment and then rinse with fresh, clean water. Do not use any other type of soap or detergent.

5.2.4 Do not use degreasing agents. such as WD 40, because they can reduce lubrication and accelerate wear by its abrasive effect.

5.2.5 Do not use water pressure machines.

5.2.6 To lubricate metal parts, use only fluid oils (engine oil type) or graphite lubricants. After lubricating, clean the excess with a cloth to prevent oil contact with the ribbons, lifelines and ropes.

6. Specific maintenance of the PPE

In the following section, some general maintenance tips are provided for each piece of equipment:

6.1 Helmets

6.1.1 Read the technical note and follow the manufacturer's recommendations at all times.

6.1.2 Do not store the helmet with equipment on it, making it pressure.

6.1.3 In case of a lot of sweat, use a handkerchief or bandana to protect it.

6.1.4 Do not personalize using stickers and chemical paints. Use only water-based glues.

6.1.5 Don't sit on the shell.

6.1.6 Wash with warm water and mild soap and no detergent. Do not use other types of soaps or detergents. Rinse with fresh water and do not dry it in the sun, Leave In the shade and in a ventilated place.

6.1.7 Do not use water pressure machines.

6.1.8 Wash helmet shell slightly with a piece of cloth and a little alcohol. Do not immerse the helmet in alcohol.

6.2 Harness

6.2.1 Read the technical note and follow the manufacturer's recommendations always.

6.2.2 An alternative is to wash the harness in a washing machine, in a soft mode or for synthetic fabrics with warm water. Do not use the drying or centrifuging stage. Place the harness in a bag so that the buckles and straps do not hit the machine.

6.2.3 To identify a harness, the user can use a small piece of adhesive tape on the comfort items or write on the label.

6.2.4 Wash the harness with lukewarm water and mild soap without detergent (PH neutral). Many products are powerful and could cause damage to the polyamide and affect the piece of equipment.

6.2.5 Then rinse thoroughly with clean water to remove soap and debris.

6.2.6 Keep the harness clean, wash regularly, allowing you to see the identification marks, serial number, dates, certifications, etc.

6.2.7 Rinse with fresh water and clean your harness after use in saline places or near the sea.

6.2.8 If you have stains, you can use a small brush to remove them.

6.2.9 Do not use pressurized water machines.

6.3 Carabiners

6.3.1 Read the technical note and follow the manufacturer's recommendations always.

6.3.2 Lubricate the gate joint if the spring does not operate automatically.

6.3.3 Lubricates the screw lock to operate freely in both directions.

6.3.4 Lubricates the automatic lock, which works according to the manufacturer's instructions.

6.3.5 After lubricating, wipe off excess with a cloth to prevent oil contact with webbing, lifelines and cordage.

6.4 Pulleys

6.4.1 Read the technical note and follow the manufacturer's recommendations always.

6.4.2 The ball bearings are already lubricated, and the bearings are self-lubricating. For this reason, a specific lubrication procedure has not been identified. In case of intensive use, you can use fluid lubricants (such as engines oils).

6.4.3 Do not use lubricants like WD-40, as the gaskets and bearings of the Pulley may be dried and damaged.

6.4.4 Do not use water pressure machines.

6.5 Ropes

6.5.1 Read the technical note and always follow the manufacturer's recommendations.

6.5.2 Keep the rope in a rope bag, without coiling them, to avoid kinks.

6.5.3 Don't step on the ropes.

6.5.4 Do not always use the same tip to

make knots or anchors/belay systems.

6.5.5 Do not rappel fast, that makes the mantle of the rope warm and accelerates the process of wear. During very fast descents, the surface can reach the melting temperature of polyamide (230 °f/110 °c).

6.5.6 Keep the ropes clean at all times. A muddy, dirty rope can prevent the descent device from working properly. A wet rope impregnated with sand dust can cause premature wear of the belay device and connectors.

6.5.7 Rinse the rope with water after use, especially in saline environments.

6.5.8 Wash the ropes with warm water and neutral soap (PH neutral). Do not use any other type of soap (solvents/stain remover/degreaser) that could damage the rope. Then rinse with fresh, clean water.

6.5.9 You can use a washing machine. Use it uses in delicate mode or for synthetic textiles. Do not use the spin mode because the centrifugal force may affect the rope.

6.5.10 Use only neutral soap. All other products are too powerful and are not compatible with polyamide.

6.5.11 Do not use water pressure machine.

6.6 Lanyards

6.6.1 Read the manufacturer's recommendations for the maintenance provided on the technical data sheet.

6.6.2 Use rope criteria's.

6.6.3 If the lanyard has an integrated connector, follow carabiner criteria's.

7. How to Identify the Equipment

To personalize a textile piece of equipment, the recommended place to write information and identify it, is on the free space that the label offers. Remember that markers, chemicals, adhesive tapes, and adhesives may not be friendly with polyamide. The effect could alter its resistance.

Metal components or equipment can be identify using an electric marker machine. In this way, you can electric mark somewhere in the Equipment that does not interfere with the information provides from its manufacture.

Unit 4
Course Components & Inspection

Inspecting the Zip Line/Canopy Tour is an integral part of the course operation. The purpose of the inspections is to ensure the integrity and functionality of the course structures and components and therefore the safety of the guides and participants. This section will describe the different types of inspections that are performed in the Zip Line/Canopy Tour and comply with the ACCT standards.

1. Types of Inspections

There are different types of inspection for Zip Line/Canopy Tour. It's important understand that the inspections are an integral risk management practice of the operation.

The different types of inspections can be divided into 2 categories:

    1.1 In-House inspections

    1.2 Professional inspections

1.1 In-House Inspections

The In-House Inspections are an indispensable task in the course operation and an ACCT standard. Through these inspections is that the needs are discovered and failures of the structures that compose the course. Failures in Canopy Tour structures can become losses and even the death of an Adventure Guide (AG) or customer. For that reason, inspections take special attention. These Categories of inspections are performed by the In-house inspector. The In-House Inspections are composed of 2 types:

    1.1.1 Periodic inspections

    1.1.2 Daily inspections

1.1.1 Periodic Inspections

The periodic inspections are those that are carried out at a certain time or periodically to determine how the conditions of the course are. This type of inspection is performed between the Professional Inspections. The frequency of periodic inspections will depend on the course design, the environmental conditions, the volume of use, and the experiences of the course staff.

1.1.2 Daily inspections

Daily inspections are performed every day that the adventure course is operated. This is the inspection that is done before starting the daily operation and indeed open the course to the public. Reasons such as vandalism, damage caused by natural elements or weather can affect the Course in less than 24 hours. The ACCT standard is clear, the elements must be free of dangers before starting operations with the public.

1.2 Professional Inspections

Certified inspections are performed by

Professional Inspectors or (a third party). Each Owner/Operator has the responsibility to contact and hire a certified inspector.

All the different types of inspections are of great importance, some do not replace the others, even more, complement each other. The professional feeds on the information documented in the local inspections. In the same way, the local inspectors are nourished by the information in the professional documents.

The certified inspections are composed of 3 types:

    1.2.1   Inspection of acceptance

    1.2.2   Professional inspections

    1.2.3   Periodic internal monitoring

1.2.1 Acceptance Inspection

The acceptance inspection is defined by the ACCT as the final inspection of the performance of a course by a qualified person, once the installation has been completed and before the commission of the same. The acceptance inspections are made to verify if in effect, the manufacture, construction, and installation of a new element or a mayor modification, was performed correctly and the Course works according to its intention.

1.2.2 Professional Inspection

The professional inspection is defined by the ACCT as an inspection by a qualified person who revises the conditions of the adventure course and identifies which areas do not meet or possibly will not comply with the standard. The Course manufacturer or a certified Inspector are responsible for conducting this type of inspection and determining the frequency to do it.

1.2.3 Periodic internal monitoring

This inspection is implemented by the organization and carried out according to the Inspector's recommendations. The purpose is to monitor and document the operation of the course.

2. Adventure Guide as an Inspector

The purpose of this manual is to introduce the AG with the basic knowledge of Course inspections. Being an inspector is a professional job that requires training time and experiences to acquire that knowledge and skills.

The AG is the employee who is actively in the course, in contact and observing the components thereof. The AG must need a basic knowledge of the components that make up the course and that minimum signals should be recognized. The purpose of this knowledge of basic inspection is that the AG while doing its work, may notice some anomaly, damage, deformity or other situation that, at first glance, show that there is a situation to be addressed. The responsibility of the AG is to notify the Operator or another employee in charge (inspector, maintenance, etc.), that there is a situation to pay attention.

3. What should the AG do when they find a suspicious component that may not pass inspection?

3.1 The adventure course must have aa policy that establishes which is the procedure with the course components that need to be inspected.

3.2 The AG verbally communicate to the employee in charge of the inspection, about the noticed situation.

3.3 Some courses have a document to report those situations. In that case, complete it.

4. <u>Course Components</u>

The adventure course specifically the Zip Line/Canopy Tour company consists of different structures, elements, Equipment, processes and technical systems. The whole Course and its components can be classified into 3 big areas; Structural, Technical systems and Zip Line Systems:

4.1 Structures

4.1.1 Pillars (wooden poles)

4.1.2 Trees

4.1.3 Anchors embedded in the ground

4.1.4 Beams

4.2 Technical Systems

4.2.1 Element Connection Systems

4.2.2 Guy cables and Critical Guy cable

4.2.3 Anchorage Systems

4.2.4 Lifeline Systems

4.3 Zip Line Systems

4.3.1 Steel Cables

4.3.2 Metal and synthetic terminations

4.3.3 Brake Systems

4.3.4 Platforms

Course Inspection

In general terms, the materials that make the Zip Line/Canopy Tour are metals, textiles, and wood. The following table shows the criteria that can be observed in each one of the different materials

Metal Components	Textile Components	Wooden Components
Deformation	Signs of Excessive Wear	Deformation
	Stains	
Signs of excessive wear	Cuts	Cracks
Rust & corrosion	Torn	Excessive play
	Chemical exposure	
Marks	Burns	Rot
Oxidation	Burrs	Pests
Grooves	Excessive fuzziness	Fungal infection
Deflection	Deformation	
Cracks	Frays	
Burrs	Glazing	
Broken wires	Pulled stitched	
	Soft & Stiff spots	

Inspection criteria in the ZIP/Line Canopy Tour components:

4.1 Structures

4.1.1   Wooden poles

4.1.1.1 Degradation of the abutment in the extremities, either in the upper tip or the area that is in contact with the ground.

4.1.1.2 Rotten parts in any part of the pillar.

4.1.1.3 Broken parts, splits, cracks or cracks either vertical or horizontal in any part of the pillar.

4.1.1.4 Some kind of damage caused by natural effects such as flora, fauna, thunderstorms, droughts, etc.

4.1.2   Trees

4.1.2.1 Damage caused by the element.

4.1.2.2 About crust growth in wood structures, screws, bolts, etc.

4.1.2.3 Damage caused by natural elements.

4.1.2.4 Damage caused by animals.

4.1.2.5 Damage from insect invasion.

4.1.2.6 Loss of leaves and foliage.

4.1.2.7 Abnormalities or changes in foliage.

4.1.2.8 Rotting of branches and/or trunk.

4.1.2.9 Loss of bark.

4.1.2.10 Signs of erosion.

4.1.2.11 Exposed roots.

4.1.2.12 Visible signs of disease due to obvious changes in the general structure of the tree, branches, and leaves.

4.1.3 Anchors embedded in the ground

4.1.3.1 Optimal operation of the anchor system.

4.1.3.2 Defects at the point of connection or anchorage point.

4.1.3.3 Steel anchor condition (Corrosion, deformations, lack of bolts, wear, etc.).

4.1.3.4 Defects in metal parts.

4.1.3.5 Condition of the wooden post in the soil (rot, cracks, etc...).

4.1.3.6 Rot

4.1.3.7 Damage to the ground surrounding the anchor.

4.1.3.8 Situations that could affect the components of the system.

4.1.4 Beams

4.1.4.1 Follow the inspection criteria recommended by the manufacturer.

4.1.4.2 Corrosion in the structure or metal parts.

4.1.4.3 Condition of the woods used.

4.1.4.4 Abrasions, unprotected areas, metals exposed.

4.1.4.5 Condition of metal joints with metal.

4.1.4.6 Condition of the bolts, screws, nuts, and washers used throughout the structure.

4.1.4.7 Welding condition.

4.1.4.8 Deformities, bends, or flexible parts.

4.1.4.9 Signs of use, wear or impact by the natural elements.

4.1.4.10 Condition of anchor points or rope connection points, lanyards, belay devices and belay systems.

4.1.4.11 Exposed sharp areas that may cause damage to an employee or participants.

4.2 Technical Systems

4.2.1 Element Connection Systems

4.2.1.1 Follow the inspection criteria recommended by the manufacturer.

4.2.1.2 Evaluate the parts of the connecting components in the elements.

4.2.1.3 Inspect the condition of the steel cable.

4.2.1.4 Inspect the conditions of the terminations.

4.2.1.5 Inspect the conditions of the synthetic and natural ropes.

4.2.1.6 Inspect the conditions of the wood components.

4.2.1.7 Inspect the conditions of the fittings.

4.2.1.8 Inspect the conditions of steel parts.

4.2.2 Guy cables and critical guy cables

4.2.2.1 Follow the inspection criteria recommended by the manufacturer.

4.2.2.2 Evaluate the conditions of the anchors and their connection points.

4.2.2.3 Inspect the conditions of the guy cables for defects, corrosion, deformities, stress, and material conditions.

4.2.2.4 Identification of natural elements that affect the guy cable.

4.2.2.5 Inspect soil conditions, especially the area surrounding the anchor.

4.2.2.6 Inspect soil conditions for erosion or exposure of the anchor system due to ground movement.

4.2.2.7 Inspect steel cable conditions (use steel wire criteria).

4.2.2.8 Inspect termination conditions (use termination criteria).

4.2.3 Anchor Systems

The following criteria are general, so they can apply to any type of anchor:

4.2.3.1 Follow the inspection criteria recommended by the manufacturer.

4.2.3.2 Inspect the conditions of use and wear.

4.2.3.3 Check the conditions of the connections with bolts, rivets, screws, nuts and washers.

4.2.3.4 Inspect for weakness.

4.2.3.5 Inspect loose parts that are not adjusted according to their manufacturing.

4.2.3.6 Inspect soil conditions, erosion, terrain movement.

4.2.3.7 Inspect signs of deterioration around bolts.

4.2.3.8 Loss of anchor components.

4.2.3.9 Loose bolts or improper movement.

4.2.3.10 Damage caused by the environment.

4.2.3.11 Chemical discoloration or effects of natural elements (sun, thunderstorms, moisture).

4.2.3.12 Condition of terminations.

4.2.3.13 Improper positioning of the components.

4.2.3.14 Distortion of steel wire strands.

4.2.3.15 Damage from the effect of the stress.

The following criteria are based on steel anchors components:

4.2.3.16 Follow the inspection criteria recommended by the manufacturer.

4.2.3.17 Inspect corrosion conditions.

4.2.3.18 Inspect conditions of the welding.

4.2.3.19 Signs of deterioration around the bolt or of the embedded material.

4.2.3.20 Abrasions, unprotected areas, metals exposed.

4.2.3.21 Loss of the surface layers of the metal by corrosion, wear or other conditions.

4.2.3.22 Damage due to overweight or the effects of voltage.

The following criteria are based on wood anchors components:

4.2.3.23 Follow the inspection criteria recommended by the manufacturer.

4.2.3.24 Signs of deterioration around screws, nuts and washers.

4.2.3.25 Growth of trees on bolts, screws, and washers.

4.2.3.26 Inspect loss of the surface layer of wood by rotting.

4.2.3.27 Condition and/or health of trees or other natural elements.

4.2.3.28 Inspect fractures or cracks in different wood components.

4.2.3.29 Damage due to overweight or stress effects.

The following criteria are based on embedded rock or concrete anchors:

4.2.3.30 Inspect according to manufacturer's recommended inspection criteria.

4.2.3.31 Inspect signs of deterioration around bolts or material embedded in rock or concrete.

4.2.3.32 Bolts removed or ejected outward or with movements.

4.2.3.33 Inspect for deteriorating conditions, fractures, cracks or flexible parts.

4.2.3.34 Inspect corrosion conditions.

4.2.3.35 Age of the components.

4.2.3.36 Inspect conditions of use and wear.

4.2.3.37 Loss of components.

4.2.3.38 Exposure or breaking of material or embedded glue.

4.2.4　Lifeline Systems

4.2.4.1 Rope inspection in its entirety length.

4.2.4.2 Outside cover condition, signs of excessive abrasion, signs of use, discoloration, soft or hard parts, changes in diameter, burns signals, or displacement of the outer cover.

4.2.4.3 Condition of the internal fibers of the rope, exposure of the internal fibers, changes in consistency when the rope is folded U-shaped.

4.2.4.4 Termination conditions at all anchorage points (use termination inspection criteria).

4.3 Zip Line Systems

4.3.1　Steel Cables

4.3.1.1 Follow the manufacturer's recommendations.

4.3.1.2 Inspect the lifeline entirety.

4.3.1.3 Inspect reductions in diameter or surface layer for loss of material, corrosion, use or wear.

4.3.1.4 Conditions or signs of fatigue.

4.3.1.5 Terminations condition (use the termination criteria).

4.3.1.6 Inspect split threads or wires, open ends, sunken or open parts.

4.3.2　Metal and synthetic terminations

4.3.2.1 Follow the recommendations of the manufacturing.

4.3.2.2 Inspect corrosion conditions, cracks,

crevices or deformities.

4.3.2.3 Inspect for proper torque.

4.3.2.4 Correct amount and space of terminations.

Ferrules for steel cables

4.3.2.5 Inspect according to the criteria of Manufacturer-Recommended inspection.

4.3.2.6 Inspect the quantity and size of the swage.

4.3.2.7 Inspect conditions of deformities, corrosion, cracks, split parts, displacement, or movements.

4.3.2.8 Inspect surface layer loss conditions, signs of wear and tear.

4.3.2.9 Inspect for broken strand before and after the ferrules.

Synthetic terminations

4.3.2.10 Inspect conditions for signs of use, age, wear or kinks.

4.3.2.11 Inspect the conditions for abrasions, cuts and broken fibers.

4.3.2.12 Inspect the correct amount and space of terminations.

4.3.2.13 Inspect discoloration conditions for exposure effects or effects of ultraviolet rays.

4.3.2.14 Inspect conditions of corrosion, cracks, cracks or deformities.

4.3.3 Brake Systems

4.3.3.1 Inspect the conditions of the steel cables and their terminations.

4.3.3.2 Inspect the conditions of the dynamic ropes and their terminations.

4.3.3.3 Inspect the conditions of the wood components.

4.3.3.4 Inspecting cushioned objects installed on the lifeline to receive and absorb impacts from Trolley systems.

4.3.3.5 Inspecting spring-type metal devices installed on the lifeline to receive and absorb impacts.

4.3.3.6 Inspect mechanical systems to catch pulleys and Trolley systems (follow manufacturer's recommendations).

4.3.3.7 Inspect the conditions of the directional pulleys.

4.3.3.8 Inspect the condition of hydraulic devices and systems (follow manufacturer's recommendations).

4.3.3.9 Inspect the condition of automatic appliances (follow manufacturer's recommendations).

4.3.4 Platforms

4.3.4.1 Inspect according to manufacturer's recommended inspection criteria.

4.3.4.2 Inspection of the conditions of the wooden structures.

4.3.4.3 Inspect wood rot and surrounding screws or bolts.

4.3.4.4 Inspection of the conditions of the bolts and screws, excess deformity of weight, signs of corrosion.

4.3.4.5 Inspect severe cracks, signs of use, degradation of wood, and deformities.

4.3.4.6 Inspect broken or cracked parts, loose or unscrewed screws, overweight hardware, hardware with screw failures.

4.3.4.7 Inspect impacts by nature, growth of tree bark on the structure, signs of impacts by thunderstorms.

4.3.4.8 Inspect damage to land foundations and damage to the structures.

Unit 5
Risk Management & The Adventure Guide

In the adventure course operation, a series of actions and processes related to risk management are performed. Many of these processes are associated with the work and responsibilities of the adventure guide (AG). In this section, you will be able to see what other functions the AG plays that are directly related to risk management. For example, equipment and course inspections, registration processes before the adventure, course operation, technical rescues and incident response, are stages and tasks within the operation based on risk management and directly related to the work and responsibilities of the AG.

1. What is Risk Management?

Risk Management is a very wide, diverse and controversial area within the Zip Line/Canopy Tours industry. Before defining it, for the purposes of this manual, risk management will be divided into two areas; An area related to the administration and operation of the Adventure Course and another area related to the work of the Adventure Guide. In practice, the management is a set of actions, but this manual is focused on the AG.

Risk management in relation to the AG can be defined as a set of practices and actions aimed to the safety of the people in their charge during the adventure experience. The risk management actions are performed before, during and after the adventure.

1.1 Some of the risk management actions that the AG must perform are:

1.1.1 Maintain constantly risk management strategies before, during and after the adventure tour.

1.1.2 Do not work outside the physical and health limits.

1.1.3 Follow rules, protocols, policies and processes related to the operation and risks management plan.

1.1.4 Provide first aid and respond to emergency situations.

1.1.5 Inform the participants about the participation requirements and perform the screening process.

1.1.6 Provide the safety talk before the adventure Tour. That the opportunity to communicate the risks before the tour.

1.1.7 Explain the responsibilities of the participants, related to risk management.

1.1.8 Communicate weather conditions for AG and customers to be prepared.

1.1.9 Maintain a risk communication with clients at all times during the adventure tour.

1.1.10 Serve as a role model for the participants through their actions and examples.

1.1.11 Keep under evaluation the performance of the clients during the experience, to make sure that they can face each elements of the course.

1.1.12 Analyze the risks throughout the whole adventure tour.

1.1.13 Prevent, mitigate, or eliminate the dangers that arise during the adventure.

1.1.14 Report and communicate accidents, incidents and dangerous areas or components of the course so that other employees know the situations and know how to handle and proceed to them.

1.1.15 Report and communicate information regarding to the Equipment conditions once inspections are performed. This prevents other AG and customers from using retired Equipment.

1.1.16 Communicate the conditions of the first aid kit to prevent other AG from using it with a lack of supplies.

2. The Guide and Risk management

The AG has the great responsibility and commitment to follow and implement the risk management practices established in the course. There are factors that can inhibit or alter the ability of the AG to analyze the risks.

For that reason, the AG must be trained to evaluate their own behaviors, actions and decisions and how they can affect their judgment and ability to analyze and manage the risks during the tour. Some of the situations or reasons that inhibit the AG from analyzing the risks:

2.1 Behavior and reaction to new and unexpected situations

Although the adventure program can be repetitive, sometimes, due to external factors, the situation or programming can change. It is important that the AG has the capacity to adjust to the new situations that arise to safeguard the safety of the participants. If the AG does not adapt to a sudden change, it will not have the ability to analyze the risks.

2.2 Egos and senses of superiority

Some AG want to attribute all the achievements, as well as highlight their knowledge and skills. At the time of an unexpected negative event, they blame the environment or other AG. This type of behavior can divert attention from the real work that the AG is to monitor and ensure the safety of the participants. That is, it can inhibit its ability to analyze the risks.

2.3 Concentration

Some AG lower their guard due to fatigue, distraction or lack of interest. In this way, the AG does not have the necessary attention to ensure, discover and analyses the risks. It is important that the AG has a good mental condition and is focused on risk management issues to avoid possible dangerous situations.

2.4 Rush and Time Management

Haste only leads to mistakes. The AG must follow the plan as it is written. It is important to consider that participants do not have the experiences or knowledge of the AG. The rush places the participant in a difficult situation, creates stress and lends himself to make mistakes in its tour.

2.5 Acceptance of risks

This phenomenon tries to explain how individuals, when they encounter the influence of others, can take on more dangerous behaviors. Regardless, it is important for the AG to maintain its behavior always. During a Tour, it is not the time to act as if they were alone and behaving in such a way, to impress others.

2.6 Poor judgment

At all times, the AG should use its judgment and experiences to analyze possible risks and dangers. It is unacceptable that the AG ignores or does not exercise its knowledge at the time of analyzing risks during the adventure program. The AG never must not be distracted, but quite the opposite, use their experiences to manage the risks and manage the program safely.

3. Accident Theory

The guide need to know from where comes the risk, and how they transform into an accident. For example, a sharp piece of metal on a trail is a danger, but it is not a risk to anyone if the AG does not use the trail because it decided to take another route to avoid that danger or the risk of someone cutting the skin with the metal. In that case, the AG handled the danger and possible risk by taking another route.

Why do accidents sometimes occur if there are alternatives to managing risks? That question can have many answers and has been the source of research for many decades.

3.1 Accidents

An accident occurs unexpectedly and without intent, and typically results in injury or deferent types of losses:

3.1.1 Physical: Wounds, illnesses, or death

3.1.2 Social: Feeling humiliated in front of a group

3.1.3 Emotional: Feeling scared

3.1.4 Financial: Losing equipment and belongings

If the AG knows the mechanism by which accidents occur, then it will have better tools to prevent them from happening. Most accidents occur when three types of hazards are combined:

3.2 Environmental influences

3.3 Participant influences

3.4 Adventure Guide influences

The AG should know and understand how to handle each factor to reduce the chance of an accident during the adventure tour:

of the dangers that come from the environment include, but are not limited to:

3.2.1 Altitude

3.2.2 Animals

3.2.3 Landslides

3.2.4 Hot or cold water

3.2.5 Water currents

3.2.6 Floods of rivers

3.2.7 Deep water

3.2.8 Branches falling from the top

3.2.9 Insects

3.2.10 Thunderstorms

3.2.11 Fire

3.2.12 Visibility

3.2.13 Climate

3.2.14 Muddy terrain

3.2.15 Snow

3.2.16 Avalanches

3.2.17 Hailstorms

3.2.18 Tornadoes

3.2.19 Marine waterspouts

3.2.20 Temperature

3.2 Environment influences: The dangers that come from the environment, no human being has control over them. In that case, the AG is responsible for studying the weather and recognizing when the adventure Tour must be canceled. When weather conditions change during the Tour, the AG must be able to make decisions such as canceling the activity, taking emergency routes, sheltering in key locations, and having the necessary Equipment for possible consequences. Some

3.3 Participant influences: Another of the variables that enhance an accident is the influence of the customers. The client can break the rules and assume attitudes and behaviors that threaten their security as they are enjoying the Tour to live new experiences and challenges.

Customers may think that risk management is not their responsibility. Unacceptable behaviors, as well as refusing to comply with documents and other processes, are grounds and signs of people who can cause accidents. Some of the dangers that come from customers include, but are not limited to:

3.3.1 Exceeding skills

3.3.2 Fall

3.3.3 Do not follow instructions

3.3.4 Hurry

3.3.5 Inadequate supervision

3.3.6 Bad examples

3.3.7 Non-effective instructions

3.3.8 Lost

3.3.9 Make Mistakes

3.3.10 Poor hygiene

3.3.11 Urine and defecation.

3.4 Adventure Guide influence: Ironically, the person who oversee ensuring the safety of the clients and managing the associated risks, sometimes assume attitudes and behaviors that do not allow them to analyze the risks. The story reveals that many of the accidents recorded in the adventure course industry occur because of human errors committed by the AG.

Some of the dangers that come from the adventure guides include, but are not limited to:

3.4.1 Assume

3.4.2 Attitudes towards risk

3.4.3 Lack of importance

3.4.4 Denial

3.4.5 Distraction

3.4.6 Erratic behavior

3.4.7 Little Stress

3.4.8 Fatigue

3.4.9 Inflexibility or reluctance to change complacency

3.4.10 Health status

3.4.11 Non-effective monitoring

3.4.12 Lack of experience

3.4.13 Lack of skills and knowledge

3.4.14 Lack of respect for the dangers

3.4.15 Don't use judgment

3.4.16 Use of intoxicating drugs and beverages.

4. Course Operation: This three variables, environment, client, and adventure guide are mixed together during adventure. From that point of view, the course and its operation is also a variable that may contributes to the emergence of an accident. For example, the AG can have optimal behavior, managing its customers and the environment, but may suffer an accident on a ladder or platforms with malfunction due to lack of maintenance.

Some of the dangers that come from the adventure course are:

4.1 Lack of inspections and maintenance.

4.2 Uninspected Steel Cables.

4.3 Platforms and stairs in bad condition

4.4 Damaged Equipment that may fail.

4.5 Condition of the ropes for belay and descent.

4.6 Fails in zip-line braking systems.

4.7 Lack of safety lanyards to anchor on platforms.

4.8 Failures in the equipment and devices that compose the course.

4.9 Failures in initial communication with the customer.

4.10 Failure of requirements, "screening" and other methods of registration and participation.

4.11 Lack of communication equipment at the course and during the adventure tours.

4.12 Failure to complete the documentation required to participate.

4.13 Absence of specialized equipment for the adventures.

4.14 Absence of first aid equipment and trained staff to bring help.

4.15 Absence of equipment for technical rescue situations.

5. Risk Management Situations

Before, during, and after the Zip Lines/Canopy Tours operation, situations may occur without prior notice. During the operational process, the guide must be aware of any failure in risk management. Failures in risk management that are not addressed, can result in an accident or an emergency situation.

There are 3 steps that the AG can perform once its detected or identifies a failure or a violation in risk management:

Step 1

Approach carefully if there is no danger, identify and make sure that in effect, there is a situation that compromises risk management.

Step 2

If it is a situation where the Guide can interact with it to eliminate the risk, act and eliminate it immediately.

Step 3

Once the Guide dealt with the situation, or if it cannot be addressed by the Guide, the next step is to inform the staff in charge to attend it. Once the situation is resolved, it is important to document it and communicate to other AG either for prevention or to have tools in case the same thing happens to them again.

Unit 6
Risk Management before Operation

1. Operating procedures before the Tour

Before the adventure Tour, the Adventure Guide (AG) will perform the following task:

1.1 Initial inspection of the Adventure Course

1.2 Preparing the Equipment

1.3 Participant Screening

1.4 Participant Requirements

1.5 Reservation Processes

1.6 Waivers

1.7 Medical History

1.8 Setting up the Client with PPE

1.9 Safety Talk

1.10 Ground School

1.11 Demonstration

1.12 Screening Decisions

1.1 Initial Adventure Course Inspection

Before opening the Canopy/Zip Line Tour to the public, the AG must make a full course cycle of all the elements that compose the course. The purpose is to make sure everything is in good condition, there is nothing to interrupt the tour, that lifelines and trails are free of obstacles and nothing that affects the security of the client.

Be sure there is no intentional damage like robbery or vandalism. There must be a template or form to document this initial inspection daily.

1.2 Preparing the Equipment

At this stage, the AG get all the equipment that customers will use. This includes rescue equipment, belay, rappelling or any other activity that is going to be performed. Risk management practice is to perform a tactile and visual inspection to the equipment. The purpose is to ensure that the equipment used in the operation, by the customer, as well as the guide equipment, is hazard-free and ready to be used. In some courses, the operation requires documenting the equipment that are used, and to have a control of the equipment that are used daily and what condition they are in.

1.3 Participant Screening

The fact that the Zip Line/Canopy Tour is a high-risk attraction, it requires establishing a participation requirement. Therefore, the AG and other employees must make sure that customers comply with the participation requirements.

The action of ensuring compliance with the requirements of participation is known as "screening". In practice, the process starts from the first customer approach to the company, Either by email, online, or by phone. It is the staff's responsibility from the beginning or from the first orientation to use the process of screening to filter individuals that do not meet the participation requirements.

Because screening in the first approach to the company may fail, it is a situation that puts responsibility in the AG. The AG must make sure that all customers meet the participation requirements. So, the screening process for AG starts from the first contact with the customer. The AG should verify data such as age, height, weight, but also should use their senses, observing and listening to realize behaviors or comments that may give the hint that might cause some type of problem or that represents a potential risk.

From that point of view, that's the moment to evaluate directly the client. It is important to consider that the Zip Line Tour possess inherent risk, makes no sense to the operation to add an additional risk. In the first contact with the customer the AG must consider this recommendation:

1.3.1 Verify that they meet all the participation requirements.

1.3.2 Keep your eyes open and observe behaviors that may represent risks.

1.3.3 Keep your ears open and listen to comments that may translate into possible risks.

1.4 Participant Requirements

All Courses have a requirement to participate. The Adventure Courses are places of high risk, for that reason, participants with certain conditions or physical characteristics, could not be suitable to perform certain activities. It is important for the AG to know what the participation requirements are, in order to run the screening process correctly. Some of the requirements usually use it in Canopy/Zip Line Tour are:

1.4.1 Completing and signing documents as the form of: registration, waivers, and medical

1.4.2 Age

1.4.3 Weight

1.4.4 Height

1.4.5 Medical conditions

1.4.6 Physical condition

1.4.7 Ability to perform course elements

1.4.8 Exclusion of certain illnesses or medical conditions.

1.4.9 Not being pregnant.

1.4.10 Wear recommended clothing and footwear.

1.4.11 Not being under the influence of drugs or alcohol.

1.4.12 Weather or environmental conditions.

1.5 Registration Processes

Once the client is in the Course, probably the first document to complete either from the AG or from the office/reception is the Participant's Registration Form. This form generally requires personal information, emergency contacts, risk management-related information, health insurance policies, and payment method. Each adventure course has its way of registering participants.

1.6 Waivers

Through this document in the form of a contract, the participant can read and learn in detail about all the risks involved in the adventure tour. Being aware, the customer may have the opportunity and the right to refuse to participate in the adventure. If the individual decides to participate, there is a document that evidences that he was oriented and warned about the risks, dangers and possible damages and losses that it could face. Like the rest of the documents, this are risk management measures and this waiver in particular, can have legal connotations in some countries.

1.7 Medical history

This document contains confidential information about diseases or medical conditions who suffer the participants. This document has traditionally been controversial, as many customers reserve the right to disclose their medical information. In general terms, if the adventure activity requires so, it is important to know some medical information about the client, which could be useful in case of an accident or emergency.

1.8 Setting up the Client with PPE

Once the client completes all the documents, usually the next step is to set him up with the Personal Protective Equipment (PPE). It is a great responsibility of the AG to set this equipment on customers.

This action has great implications for risk management because if the PPE fails, the consequences could be the loss of a life. Then, fitting the helmet correctly, adjusting the harness appropriately and connecting parts of Equipment in the correct way, are part of the tasks and responsibility who have the AG.

The PPE consists of:

1.8.1   Helmet

1.8.1.1 The helmet must be straight, covering the front head of the participant.

1.8.1.2 Properly adjusted so that it does not have movement when the customer moves, fit it to the sides and from the bottom to the top.

1.8.1.3 Webbing of the chinstrap must be adjusted correctly.

1.8.1.4 Webbing must be properly fit before and after the ear.

1.8.1.5 Ensure that webbing is not bent or twisted.

1.8.2   Harness

1.8.2.1 The webbing of the waist should be above the hips and adjusted as much as possible without causing damage to the customer.

1.8.2.2 Make sure that the webbing of the legs below the buttocks and that they are tight enough without causing damage to the client.

1.8.2.3 The connection point should be centered on the participant or aligned with the navel.

1.8.2.4 Make sure that the rest of the adjustment slings are properly adjusted.

1.8.2.5 If the locking buckles are automatic, make sure they are properly closed.

1.8.2.6 Make sure all buckles have the double safety back.

1.8.2.7 Accommodate all leftovers from webbing that are not hanging and may become entangled.

1.8.3   Chest Harness

1.8.3.1 Chest harness is properly adjusted. The front connection point is adjusted in the center of the chest (in the sternum) and the central point of the back is centralized among the shoulders blades.

1.8.3.2 If you move the webbing to pass over the shoulders, means that need adjustment enough to not get over them.

1.8.3.3 The chest harness is properly connected to the waist harness specifically through the points of connection manufactured by the manufacturer.

1.8.3.4 The piece of equipment (webbing, accessory cord, carabiner) uses to connect the chest harness to the Trolley system, it must be properly connected.

1.8.3.5 Make sure that the rest of the slings are properly adjusted.

1.8.3.6 If the locking buckles are automatic, make sure they are properly closed.

1.8.3.7 Make sure all buckles have the double safety back.

1.8.3.8 Accommodate all leftovers from webbing that are not hanging and may become entangled.

1.8.4   Carabiner

1.8.4.1 Make sure that all carabiner are connected properly.

1.8.4.2 Check that it is positioned properly before use it.

1.8.4.3 The carabiner is position in such a way that the weight falls on the mayor axis, not at the door.

1.8.4.4 Make sure the gate is properly closed.

1.8.4.5 If the carabiner is screw lock, check that it is closed correctly and positioned so that the thread closes downward.

1.8.4.6 If the carabiner is automatic, check that the gate is correctly locked.

1.8.5   Trolley system

1.8.5.1 Verifies that the Trolley system is connected to the harness correctly.

1.8.5.2 Make sure all the parts that compose the Trolley system, are connected correctly to each other (lanyards, carabiners, and pulleys).

1.8.5.3 Check that all carabiners that make up the Trolley system are closed and functioning properly.

1.8.5.4 If you use knots, make sure they are done correctly.

1.8.6   Lanyards

1.8.6.1 Make sure each participant has an independent lanyard connected to the Trolley system.

1.8.6.2 Check that the lanyard is properly connected to the harness.

1.8.6.3 Verifies that the lanyard has the correct connector.

1.8.7   Gloves

1.8.7.1 Make sure all participants have gloves.

1.8.7.2 Verify that all customers have gloves according to the size of their hands.

1.8.7.3 Check that the gloves cover their hands complete including fingers.

1.8.7.4 Make sure the glove is not broken or has a hole.

1.8.7.5 Check the part of the palm (which is in contact with the steel wire) has the double protection or a friction component.

1.8.7.6 Make sure that the friction component of the glove is not broken.

1.8.8 PPE Safety Check

In the start, the AG set the PPE to the customer. As time passes, the customer walks, sits and climb among other movements, so it's possible that the PPE becomes loose. This brings an implication for the risk management and the tasks of the AG.

The AG must check the PPE at all times in order prevent an accident. There are places or key moments during the operation to check the clients PPE.

At the time of checking the PPE, use the inspection criteria for each of the independent parts to ensure that all the equipment are properly installed and adjusted. Also, the guide must check if there has been any

damage to the equipment from the moment it was installed on the participant. It is highly recommended to check the PPE in the following instances:

1.8.8.1 In the first moment that the PPE is set on the client.

1.8.8.2 After the walk to the first element.

1.8.8.3 Prior to make each one of the elements.

1.8.8.4 After walking between each element.

1.8.8.5 Before connecting it to a belay system.

1.8.8.6 If you stand a long time in the heights.

1.8.8.7 If the participant leaves the tour and comes back.

1.8.8.8 After any situation that the AG creates prudent.

At the time of verifying the PPE of the client, the AG must verify:

1.8.8.9 Helmet

1.8.8.10 Chest Harness

1.8.8.11 Waist Harness

1.8.8.12 Carabiners

1.8.8.13 Lanyards

1.8.8.14 Trolley System

1.8.8.15 Gloves

1.9 Safety talk

Once the client is ready with the equipment, it is time to offer the orientation or safety talk. The purpose is to verbally warn of the risks and experiences that are about to live. Another great connotation that has this safety talk is that it has a greater impact than the AG simply reading them in a document.

1.9.1   <u>Safety Talk General Points:</u>

1.9.1.1   Provide the opportunity for the customer to listen and ask questions.

1.9.1.2   Communicate risks clearly and not with specialized vocabulary. It is important that all customers understand the message that is intended to communicate.

1.9.1.3   Describe the course, explains how long it will be, what types of elements are going to experience, the amount and level of difficulty.

1.9.1.4   If there are walks between the elements, explains the duration and the type of terrain.

1.9.1.5   Explain the importance of not having any medical condition of those identified in the participation requirements.

1.9.1.6   Explain that they cannot have any medical condition or disease that may occur or worsen for the participation on the tour.

1.9.1.7   Advise them to carry any necessary medication.

1.9.1.8   Explain how to wear their hair, dress, and advise.

1.9.1.9   Warn that they should not possess anything loose in the mouth like a candy, which can be swallowed by mistake.

1.9.1.10 You can't smoke during the adventure.

1.9.1.11 Explains the ecosystem, animals, and plants that are toxic and could affect the participants.

1.9.1.12 Explains the weather and advises the use of extra water if necessary.

1.9.1.13 Explains that if they decide to participate they are accepting the risks. In addition, there are risks that cannot be seen or prevented, so they can be surprising.

1.10 Ground School

In some courses after offering the Safety Talk, participants are led to the Ground School. The purpose is to provide the opportunity to practice techniques, movements, positions and handle some pieces of Equipment before going to the adventure. In fact, in some Courses, the Ground School is used for Screening. The AG has the opportunity of directly evaluate the customer and if they cannot master the technics or Equipment, it's time to deny their participation.

On the other hand, there are courses that either by the number of participants or because the time is compromised, it is not possible to provide the opportunity to practice. In that scenario, the AG make a demonstration.

1.10.1 Ground School General Recommendations

1.10.1.1 Explain to participants what their responsibilities during the tour are.

1.10.1.2 Teach them what are the risks, dangers and common mistakes to avoid them.

1.10.1.3 Show the proper use of the equipment.

1.10.1.4 Shows the position and orientation of the body in the zip lines.

1.10.1.5 Given the opportunity to practice skills and demonstrate that they are able to execute them.

1.10.1.6 Show them the signs, communication, and language to communicate in the zip lines.

1.10.1.7 Describes the handbrake process.

1.10.1.8 Explain how the emergency brake works.

1.10.1.9 Explain the take-off and landing procedures.

1.10.1.10 Teach auto-rescue procedures.

1.10.1.11 If the client cannot perform the techniques, skills, positions or movements, he/she will not be able to participate in the tour.

1.10.2 Parts of the Ground School

Equipment

1.1.2.1 Show them what kind of equipment they use and their names.

1.1.2.2 Explain that the equipment cannot be disconnected at any time

Positions

1.1.2.3 Explain how to sit down completely in the harness and incline backwards.

1.1.2.4 Show how to position hands.

1.1.2.5 Show how to position legs during the traverse.

1.1.2.6 Explain the position of the hands to take control of the body.

Signals

1.1.2.7 Show them the manual signals or verbal commands, when they are used and what their mean. For example: hand signals or verbal command for:

    A. Take off

    B. Land

    C. Break

    D. Do not stop, continue…

A. Take-off Platform

1.1.2.8 Explain platform rules e.g. How many people, always connected, not jumping, not smoking, etc.

1.1.2.9 Explain how to connect the lanyard in bridges and platforms.

1.1.2.10 Explain and demonstrates the position to exit the platform.

1.1.2.11 If different platforms have different positions and moves, specifies which one is performed in each of them.

1.1.2.12 Explain the position of the hands.

1.1.2.13 Be sure to explain how to slow down and let the customer know how to run it.

1.1.2.14 Clarify any questions.

B. Landing Platform

1.10.15 Explain how to connect your lanyard when land on the platform.

1.10.16 Explain and demonstrate which are the position to land on the platform.

1.10.17 Explain in which platforms it is necessary lift the feet and knees to land and when it is necessary to land with the feet.

1.10.18 If different platforms have different landing methods, make sure to explain each of them.

1.10.19 Explain the position of the hands at the time of landing.

1.10.20 Explain what to do if don't reach to the platform.

1.10.21 Explain what if when get to the platform, return back.

C. Brake

1.10.22 Explain and demonstrate the proper way of braking.

1.10.23 Take into consideration that different zip lines could have different techniques. Be sure to explain each of them.

1.10.24 Explain where the primary brake and how to activate it.

1.10.25 Explain how the emergency brake works, if applicable.

D. Self-Rescue

1.10.26 Explains how to auto-rescue if stop in the middle of the cable or get to the platform and return back.

1.10.27 Explains what technique to use for auto-rescue.

1.10.28 The basic technique is to turn on your back and push your hand over your head until you reach the platform.

At the time of showing and teaching customers the techniques, methods and positions, be sure to demonstrate clearly. That everyone can see and understand the techniques. Provides space so you can ask questions on doubts. Provides the space for practice and understand the techniques. If after a period of practice, the client is not able to perform the proven techniques, it will be necessary to cancel their participation.

1.11 Demonstration

For some reasons such as the number of participants and the time of operation, there may not be time for all participants to practice at the Ground School. In that case, a demonstration is made. The demonstration allows everyone to see the techniques and Equipment they will have to use later in the Tour.

During the Demonstration, participants can be taught with all the points of the Safety Talk and those of the Ground School. In this way, at least the participants will have a notion of what they have to do when they arrive at the first platform.

After the demonstration and ask if anyone has a question, the group will be ready to start with the Adventure Tour

1.12 Screening Decisions

It may be the case in which the participant does not meet the requirements to participate in the Tour. The reason may be age, weight, medical condition or not a satisfactorily demonstrated at the Ground School.

In that case, the participant must be informed that will not be able to participate in the tour.

Communicating that decision could be a difficult situation. Even more when the participant had the expectation of participating in the tour. Let the decision be communicated by the operator, he is the person in charge of the Course. If the decision has to be offered by the AG, follow the following recommendations:

1.12.1   Treat the participant with respect

1.12.2   Explain the reasons

1.12.3   Remind him/her that there are participation requirements

1.12.4   If necessary, give a copy of the rules or direct them to a sign that shows it

1.12.5   Do not give the decision in front of other participants

1.12.6   Shows compassion and respect when announcing the decision

1.12.7   Do not enter into discussions that could end up with major problems.

Unit 7
Risk Management during Operation

Zip Line Operation

Once the ground school is over and if customers met the requirements, they are ready to start the Zip Line/Canopy Tour. This section will be called "during the tour" and consists of all the processes that take place in the Tour once the clients pass the initial stage. Each course is different, so these steps must be adapted for each course and there may be steps that are not covered in this manual.

1. Risk Management Element Communication

From the first and in each of the elements of the course, the AG has the task and responsibility to inform the customers, the specific instructions, as well as the risks and dangers present. Of course, the participant was provided with the safety talk, Ground School and possibly demonstration but that is not enough. A risk management practice is to understand that customers are not professionals and are possibly enjoying their vacation or a day of outdoor recreation.

This information can be lost by participants in the way to the first Element, be it a zip line, a bridge or some type of aerial obstacle, climbing or Rappelling. The connotation for risk management is that the AG should reinforce customer knowledge about what it needs to know or do to cross the High Element. For that reason, there must be a risk management communication in each of the elements. In general, the AG should inform the participant about:

1.1 Where to anchor and remember that must be connected by the Layard at all times.

1.2 How to take-off from the platform.

1.3 The position of the body and control during the zip.

1.4 How to orient the body during the zip.

1.5 The position of the hands during the zip.

1.6 Visual and/or verbal signals to slow down.

1.7 How to brake.

1.8 How to land on the platform.

1.9 Depending on the course, do not touch or dismount any piece of equipment.

1.10 How to connect their lanyards on the bridges Belay cables.

1.11 If necessary, provide instructions for the next element, route by trail, aerial bridges, or transfers.

1.12 It is important to remember to the AG that the instructions should be repeated in all elements.

2. Zip Line Operation Communication Guide

Communication between the guides and clients is vital during the operation. There are several ways in which the Guides are traditionally communicated. Of all possible alternatives, the radio is the most recommended. Of course, there are places where the radios don't work. In that case, the operator must look for an alternative that is efficient for communicating and manage the risks during the operation.

Alternative communication methods must be part of the Operation Manual, in other words, a method accepted to be used during the operation. The same way, the method to communicate with the client has to be established in the Operation Manual. That's mean that exists basically two types of communications; Communication between the AG and the communication between the guide and the participant.

3. Zip Line Operational Communication Between Guides

The recommended methods of communication during the Zip Line/Canopy Tour operation are:

3.1 Radio Communication

3.2 Visual Communication

3.3 Verbal Communication

3.1 Radio Communication

Before starting the Tour, it is important to verify 2 things; Radios condition & functionality, and Clear communication between the AG is properly coordinated:

3.1.1 Radios condition & functionality

3.1.1.1 Check if the radio turns on, has charged batteries and if it has other components such as extra battery, accessory cord or carabiner to hang it, ear set and pouch, or waterproof cover.

3.1.1.2 Verify that the radio transmits and receives by testing with the Tour partner.

3.1.2 Clear communication between the AG is properly coordinated

3.1.2.1 Before you start the Tour make sure the radios are working and you have a clear communication with the other AG that will be part of the tour.

3.1.2.2 If you have any questions, if the companion guide heard the message, come back and confirm before acting. You cannot assume that he heard you or that you were answered if there is any doubt.

3.1.2.3 The Operating Manual must establish which Radio channels to communicate in the event of an emergency. If the operator assigns a radio channel to any AG, it must remain there, until he received other guidelines.

3.1.2.4 If the Course protocol requires each AG to use a radio, make sure you have one before you go to start your work.

3.1.2.5 During the Tour, check that the radio stays on and that the volume is not turned down.

3.1.2.6 If the radio stops working, try to find communication with another guide or staff, to replace it

Basic Radio Signals to Communicate between Zip Lines

Situation	Take-Off Platform Command	Landing Platform Command
The guide at the take-off platform is ready to zip the participant.	Ready "*Guide name, Nickname, number, etc.*"	
The Guide at the landing platform is ready to receive.		Ready to Zip!!
The Guide at the landing platform is not ready to receive.		Stop!!

3.2 Visual Communication

3.2.1 Hand Signal

It is not recommended that hand signals be the first option. But, there are courses with relatively short distances, where the hand signals could be used. An example of basic manual signals is the following:

3.2.2 Ready to Send

The guide at the Take-off platform puts his arm and hand in hand brake position. This signal does not require movement, just put the arm in position.

3.2.3 <u>Ready to Receive</u>

The guide on the landing platform positions its arm and hand on top of the helmet. This signal does not require movement, just put its arm in position.

3.2.4 <u>Stop</u>

The guide on the landing platform will make this sign spreading horizontally his arms. This sign means that he is not ready to receive the participant. This signal does not require movement, just put its arms in position.

3.2.5 <u>Emergency</u>

Either one of the two guides (Take-Off or landing), they'll make this signal crossing the arms like an X shape above the head it the forehead level, In case of an emergency. This signal does not require movement, just put its arms in position.

3.3 Verbal Communication

In some courses, verbal communication is used to operate the zip lines. To choose this method, it is necessary to make sure that according to the distance of the zip lines, the sound is clear, so that it can be received by the AG in both directions.

In fact, verbally you could do the same commands of radio communication, the nature of the individual seeks shorter and more precise words to make verbal communication.

In this case and usually the same sound is used for the confirmation of the participant launch. In case that the guide at the landing platform is not ready to receive, simply do not answer the sound. Silence or no answer means that the guide is not ready to receive.

Verbal Commands

Situation	Take-Off Platform Command	Landing Platform Command
The guide at the take-off platform is ready to Zip the participant.	Kukuuuuuuuu!!!	
The guide at the landing platform is ready to receive.		Kukuuuuuuuu!!!
The guide at the landing platform is **not** ready to receive.		does not answer

4. Guide to Participant Communication

The second type of communication that is used during the operation of the zip lines is the one that occurs between the Guide and the Participant. It is the responsibility of the Guide to explain and clarify all the doubts of the participant before being launched through the zip line. This information includes making sure that the participant knows the visual signs that the Guide will make on the landing platform.

Once the participant is launched through the zip line, the guide on the take-off platform basically loses visual contact with the participant. In this case, the guide on the landing platform is the one that is in a better position to communicate visually with the participant who is heading in front of him. In this case, the communication between the guide and the participant is visual. Of course, in Zip Line/Canopy Tour with relatively short distances, perhaps voice commands could also be effective.

4.1 Visual Communication

It is extremely important that all guides use the same signals, you do not want customers to be confused with different signals.

4.2 Brake Hand Signal

The guide on the landing platform makes this signal to alert the participant to start to break down.

4.2.1   The receiving staff makes this signal when he/she determines it is appropriated for the participant to brake.

4.2.2   Extend one arm out in front of the body, below the chest, with the palm side of the hand facing down and gestures downward in a pushing motion.

4.3 No-Braking Hand Signal

4.3.1   This signal alert participant to keep moving, not break or quit breaking if they are doing so.

4.3.2   The participant receives this signal for three reasons:

4.3.2.1   They should keep moving with the momentum they have and not apply their break to be able to make it to the landing area.

4.3.2.2   They have applied too much pressure while braking and have slowed down too much.

4.3.2.3   They have applied the brake incorrectly and increase risk of injuring themselves. In this case the participant will not brake themselves and the receiving staff should be prepared to operate the emergency brake.

Extend one arm out in front of the body, above the head, with the palm side of the hand facing backwards and gestures in a "come on" motion.

4.4 Speed Slow Down

This signal is used when the participant is required to decelerate but not brake completely.

5. Verbal Communication

73

The voice commands with the participants during their traversing are limited to the distance in which the participant is crossing the zip line. It is important to consider that the voice commands can be accompanied by the visual commands.

Because of the distance, the voice command is generally effective in the following situations:

Situation	Landing Platform Command
The participant is required to brake.	!!! Brake
The guide at the landing platform is ready to receive.	Kukuuuuuuuu!
The guide on the landing platform is not ready to receive.	does not answer
The participant is slowing down, and the guide asks him to release it.	Let's Go!

6. Installing Trolley

The pulley used for zip lines is usually known as Trolley. This can be used for a single cable or lifeline and in other courses when using a double lifeline, the trolley will have to be composed in a system to be able to connect to the double line.

6.1 Simple Trolley

The type of pulley is usually manufactured with fixed side plates, so that its side plates do not have movement. The procedure for installing it is as follows:

6.1.1   Slide the pulley on the side of the anchor point and insert the steel wire or rope into it.

6.1.2   Once the cable or rope is inside the pulley, place a carabiner at the anchor point.

6.1.3   The carabiner also serves as a connection point for the Trolley's life-end.

6.2 Single Trolley with single lanyard

This is the most basic configuration that can be assembled. A lanyard in a pulley. The other end of the lanyard is connected to the user's harness. In addition, you can see the independent lanyard connected to the lifeline and positioned on the pulley.

6.3 <u>Single Trolley with asymmetric double lanyard</u>

This is a configuration used in Canopy Tours with a single lifeline. In this case. the double asymmetrical lanyard is used. In this configuration the short side is connected to the Trolley and the long side to the lifeline, and the carabiner is positioned on the Trolley.

7. Installing Trolley Systems

There are a wide variety of configurations to create trolley systems. Basically, the number of lifelines, the separation between them, their size and configuration will influence the type of trolley to be used. Therefore, each course, according to its manufacturing and components, configures the most suitable trolley system. Next, several commonly used trolley systems are presented:

7.1 <u>Double Trolley with asymmetric double lanyard</u>

This is a basic configuration with an asymmetric lanyard for a double vertical lifeline (one line above the other).

One characteristic of this system is that the asymmetrical lines are connected to the carabiners in such a way that the trolley system can be installed without having to disconnect the asymmetrical lines. In other words, they stay connected all the time, so the system is always installed.

7.2 Double Trolley with asymmetrical double lanyard with connector

This is a configuration with a double asymmetrical lanyard for dual lifeline. Unlike the settings shown previously, the long line of the trolley lanyard is connected independently with a carabiner.

In some courses they use this configuration to be able to use the long line as a lanyard to connect it to an anchor point on the course. However, it is highly recommended that an independent lanyard be used.

7.3 Double Trolley with single lanyard

This is a basic configured with a simple lanyard, for double lifeline. Unlike the previous model, this system is configured with a simple sling also known as "runners". In this case, to install both pulleys it is necessary to connect them to each other with a carabiner and the simple sling on the lower pulley with another carabiner. In the lower pulley, you can see the independent safety lanyard.

7.4 Double Trolley with "Y" symmetrical Lanyard

In some Courses, the manufacturing of the lifelines are next to each other (horizontal).

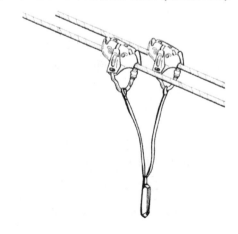

That's not a usual combination, but in fact, some courses use it. A double symmetrical lanyard is required for this configuration. In this case, the lines of the lanyard must measure the same size, to connect both pulleys.

7.5 <u>Launching of customers in the zip lines</u>
There are a number of processes when the AG receives a participant on the platform to be connected to the Trolley system and launched through the zip line. The basic steps are as follows:

1. Connect the participant's lanyards to the an anchor point
2. Install the Trolley system
3. Connect the Trolley system to the participant.
4. To install the Trolley system in some cases a step is needed so that the participant can take a higher step. In other courses the exit is to low so that the participant could even touch the platform with their butts.
5. In these types of cases, it is important for the AG to provide the correct instructions for each element.
6. Explain to the participant how to do the handbrake system, what are the brake signals and what are the positions to assume during the traverse.
7. Before sending the participant, perform a general evaluation of the Equipment, their connections and alert level of the participant before sending them, using the TLC's system.

8. TLC's

The TLC system recognizes the importance of the AG ensuring that the participant is properly connected and protected before sending through the zip line. This system was developed by Aire Libre Inc. and its objective is to provide the AG with an easy method to corroborate all the connection points of the Trolley system, as well as the lucidity of the participant before sending him to the zip line.

This is a process that the AG should do in just seconds to verify that, in fact, all points are correctly connected, and verify that the client is ready to zip. Internalizing this method needs time and practice, but once achieved, it can serve as a security alert before sending customers through zip lines.

The step before sending the client through the zip line is for use the TLC system. By saying that word, with your eyes and with an evaluation and analysis mindset, you will evaluate each of the acronym's letters, in the Trolley parts and the participant.

8.1 <u>System TLC's</u>
The TLC system consists of the following letters and parts:
T – Trolley System

T – Trolley Lanyard

L – Lanyards

C – Connections on Harness

C – Condition of the Participant

At the right time before launching the client by the zip line, the AG makes the following process:

T – Trolley System

Look at the Trolley. Certifies that the pulley (s) is installed on the lifelines correctly. If the system is a dual lifeline, check that the pulleys are correctly connected to each other. Check that all carabiners are connected to the pulleys correctly

T- Trolley Lanyard:

Observe the safety lanyard of the Trolley system, either single or double. Certifies that it is properly connected to the pulley (s) and harness. Check that all carabiners are connected to the lanyard properly

L -Safety Lanyard:

Observe the safety lanyard or independent lanyard. Certifies that the carabiner is properly connected to the harness with a carabiner or a Girth Hitch knot and at the other end to the Trolley at the appropriate location.

C - Connections on Harness

Observe the participant's harness, especially the connection point. Certifies that, in effect, the harness has two (2) pieces connected or one (1) piece and one (1) knot at its connection point. (1) The carabiner of the Trolley system, lanyard and (2) The additional lanyard carabiner or a Girth Hitch knot.

C – Condition of the Participant

The AG must make sure that the customer is in his five senses, alert, awake and aware of what he is about to do, before launching it. Before you send him, touch their helmet (to make sure you have the participant alert). You can gently touch the helmet like knocking on a door, "knock-knock." Asks him a question as a strategy to measure their level of alert before sending him, something like *Are you ready*? Or *What are you about to do?*

9. Body position

There are certain positions that individuals must assume at the time of launching by zip line. In order to assume the right body position, other aspects such as the orientation and control of the body, as well as the speed control, enter the formula. The distance of the zip line, the type of lanyard, the weight of the participant and the wind, are factors that affect the position of the participant. Here are some of the basic positions used in the Zip Line/Canopy Tour:

9.1 Zip Lines with waist harness position

The most basic way to zip line is to use a waist harness. The harness creates positions that vary depending on the weight and body shape of the user. Generally, the thinner the user, the more seated and upright he or she will be positioned. The waist harness, being placed in the middle of the body, allows a wide range of motion. This allows the customer to enjoy the natural elements and provides flexibility with the position of the hands and body in general.

9.2 Positions with waist harness

1. Brake hand position
2. Aerodynamic position
3. Kite or bat position
4. Cannonball position
5. Tandem position

9.3 Types of harness that cause other positions

1. Zip lines with waist harness and chest harness
2. Full Body Harness
3. Beach Chair
4. Superman

9.4 Handbrake position

In the courses that it is necessary to use the technique of Hand Break, the participant will have to assume that position when the AG indicates it or since it takes off the platform.

The length of the trolley system lanyard will dictate that you will have to stretch your hand to reach the cable. Young participants and children could have mishap reaching the lifeline. Assuming this position requires the participant to straighten his/her back to be able to grasp the lifeline satisfactorily and at the same time be able to close the hand to provoke the brake. The wind, speed, and weight of the participant could add some difficulty to this task.

9.5 Aerodynamic position

In some zip lines the aerodynamic position is used. This position allows the participant to cut the wind and for that reason, it is used when it is necessary to traverse quickly to reach the landing platform. In this position the participant accommodates his body upright and straight with his straight hands in the trolley system and his feet together and straight as possible.

9.6 Kite position

In Courses with fast zip lines, sometimes a position is used to create resistance to the wind and to help in the task of lowering the speed of the participant. In this case, the position of the kite or the bat is made. In this position, the participant opens and expands his legs and spleens to create a lot of surface area and collide with the wind. Hopefully, that will help a little to slow down the participant's speed.

9.7 Cannonball position

Another position that has been used when you want to traverse fast is the cannonball. In this case, the client raises his knees to his chest and hugs them with his arms to shrink and form a ball. It is important to bend your back

and head in the direction of your knees. With luck, the cannonball will traverse at high speed.

9.8 Tandem position

Another position that takes place in the Zip Line Tours is to send two customers together or tandem. Customers are in tandem because:

9.8.1   It is the philosophy and goal of the course, to launch United customers or parents with their children.

9.8.2   When an adventure guide must be launched with the customer for some security or logistical reason.

9.8.3   When the wind blows against the zip line, more dough (weight) is needed to achieve higher speed and reach the arrival platform.

9.8.4 There is no official standard on how to assemble a tandem system. Some recommendations are as follows:

9.8.4.1 Each participant must use its own trolley system.

9.8.4.2 Do not connect two customers in the same trolley system.

9.8.4.3 While assembling the system, make sure that the participants are connected to an anchor point.

9.8.4.4 Install each participant's trolley system independently.

9.8.4.5 The participant in the rear should do the handbrake if necessary.

9.8.4.6 The participant in the back could hug the participant in the front with his legs.

9.8.4.7 Each course must decide according to its operation if the participants in tandem position are connected between. For example, in some courses there is a risk that the participants will separate and then they can collide later. In this type of case, they must be connected to each other using a sling connected in their respective trolley systems.

9.8.4.8 In another type of situation, participants are not connected to each other so that they are free of movement if any situation occurs.

Each operator will have to evaluate that practice, in case of a situation,
It may be desirable for participants to be able to move independently and not connected to each other.

10. Other types of harness that cause other positions

10.1 <u>Zip lines with waist harness and chest harness</u>

The purpose of the chest harness is to support the upper part of the body. In this case, all the participants, especially the heaviest, can rest and enjoy the traverse. One advantage of the chest harness is that the user is left with their hands free to break, take pictures, self-rescue or any other task.

10.2 <u>Full Body Harness</u>

This type of harness is designed for use with fall arrest protection systems and, it has been used in some courses with great success. The type of course, its elements, and other components may require this type of harness to be used to protect the participant and the guide. Unlike the waist harness, the full body doesn't allow much movement, so you're practically in a single position.

10.3 <u>Beach Chair</u>

The long, fast zip lines that are usually manufactured with only one lifeline use this type of harness. To enjoy that experience, some companies have manufactured a harness like a beach chair. In other words, the position of the user is seated in a kind of chair that has a harness. This type of harness connects to the Trolley and becomes a manufactured seat for long zip line traverses.

10.4 Superman

The lying position or "Superman", like the beach chair, has been very popular in the Curses that have long zip lines. The system consists of a kind of harness in the form of "Peto" in which the user lies down and connects the sling system of the harness and, at the same time, the pulley system.

11. Understanding Zip Lines Brake

There are many brake systems to be used in zip line tours. Systems range from gravity braking to sophisticated mechanical brakes. The purpose of the brake system is to decelerate and reduce the speed of the participant. The brake must work without deforming or damaging the system and braking the participant regardless of the position. In addition, the brake cannot be an impediment when connecting to the lifeline and perform rescues.

There are two types of brakes:

11.1   Primary brakes

11.2   Emergency brakes.

11.1 Primary Brakes

A primary brake is defined as the main brake in a zip line brake system, engaged during normal operation to arrest a user's motion. Primary braking systems are divided into two categories: Active and Passive. It is important to highlight the fact that a brake system is passive or active in relation to the customer and not to the AG.

11.1.1 Active

-   Gravity and handbrake - the participant uses his gloved hand to create friction on the steel wire and decelerate in the landing area. The handbrake is accompanied by the effect of gravity.
-   Gravity and foot landing - Gravity slows down the participant at a reasonable speed to be able to strike on the platform until it slows down and stop.

11.1.2 Passive

This type of brake does not involve the action of the participant because they are operated by the AG. This type of brake can be either a primary or an emergency.

11.1.3 Automatic

This type of brake do not require participant or AG intervention because it works automatically. It can be a primary or emergency brake.

11.1.4 Gravity

This type of brake does not require participant action or emergency brakes. Gravity slows down the participant in a natural way.

11.2 Emergency Brakes

Emergency brakes operate automatically, do not need the activation or intervention of the participant to work. An emergency brake is defined as "a break located on a zip line that engages without any participant input upon failure of the primary break to prevent serious injury or death".

Brake techniques and methods used in the Zip Line/Canopy Tours

Type of Brake	Category	Description
Gravity Break	Primary Break	Passive to the participant Participant slow down and stop in a natural way Does not need emergency break
Hand Break	Primary Break	Active for the participant It cannot be used as an emergency brake Requires the use of gloves Require participant control y coordination
Opposable Break	Emergency Break	Passive for the participant Only for Emergency Breaks Require coordination and control to manage Hand Break Requires operator to wear gloves on both hands
Zip Stop	Primary Break	Automatic break Passive to the participant/Guide

11.2.1 Gravity Brake

In this type of brake, no action is required from the participant or the Guide. The participant must land in a controlled way on the platform. The first action of the Guide when receiving the participants must be to connect their lanyard at the correct anchor point.

11.2.2 Brake Hand

Type of active brake where the participant's intervention, using his hand with gloves, slows his movement causing friction between his hand and the lifeline.

11.2.2.1 As soon as the guide indicates, the participant must arrange the hand on the lifeline, lower cable in case of a double line.

11.2.2.2 The hand should be placed on the cable without exerting any abrupt pressure immediately. Gradually and with control, it begins to lower the hand with gloves on the lifeline to begin to create friction to decelerate.

11.2.2.3 Remember that the body is moving, you must assume a good posture to perform the Hand Break.

11.2.2.4 For any reason put the hand in front of the pulley when it is in motion.

11.2.3 Opposable Point Break (OP Break)

Type of passive brake, composed with ropes with a change of direction system that creates an opposite movement in the rope. In this way, the brake operator could pull the rope to activate or move the brake block to a point away from the platform. By being hit by the participant and moving the brake block towards the landing platform, it creates the counting effect on the AG rope. This situation allows the guide to use his hands with gloves to create friction on the rope and slow down the brake block and at the same time the participant.

OP Break operation:

11.2.3.1 Pull the brake rope so that the brake block is positioned at the breaking point.

11.2.3.2 Check that the rope is aligned, no tangles.

11.2.3.3 Make sure there are no participants in the operating area of the platform.

11.2.3.4 The Guide should keep both hands on the braking rope at all times.

11.2.3.5 This is an emergency brake; the AG must be attentive in case the participant does not stop.

11.2.3.6 When the participant hits the brake block, the AG has to apply friction with his gloved hands on the braking rope.

11.2.3.7 It is not advisable to grasp and stop the rope completely. This could create an immediate braking because the participant could be driven back.

11.2.3.8 Use the brake in such a way that you can slow down and stop the participants in a controlled way.

11.2.3.9 When the participant is on the landing platform, the first step of the AG must be to connect its lanyard to an anchor point.

11.2.4 Automatic Brake

The automatic brakes, as well its name is concerned, operate in an automatic way. It is passive for both the participant and the Guide. Generally, this type of brake is composed of a technological device where the participant collide with the brake block, releases a controlled tape that slows the participant until braking it. Once the participant is disassembled, the tape is automatically collected on the spool and is again ready for the next participant.

12. Landing Protocol

Every time a participant is traversing on a zip line, at some point he will have to make a landing on the landing platform. Landings may vary from Course to Course, some of the factors that affect are:

12.1 The speed of traversing.

12.2 The height of the lifeline in relation to the platform

12.3 The distance between the lifelines

12.4 The platform

12.5 Type of brake

The ACCT defines the landing platform as the area provided for arresting (braking) and dismounting after crossing the element. Taking that definition into consideration, the platforms must provide adequate and secure space for the customer and the AG to operate and manage the brake.

The AG must provide the participant with instructions on how to land before sending through the zip line. As you approach the landing platform, the Guide receiving will make a visual or vocal signal to alert when the participant must perform the action or assume the position for landing. The AG on the landing platform cannot explain the process, it only provides the signal from when to perform the action. For that reason, it takes great importance for the Guide at the take-off to ensure that the participant knows the landing process before sending him.

13 Dismount

Dismount is the process that occurs when the participant lands on the platform. ACCT defines it as the act of disembarking from an element and proceeding away from the landing area. For this process the AG must know which Is the operating process on the landing platform.

Each course can have a different process, but in general terms the following actions are performed:

13.1   Once the participant lands, the first action is to connect his lanyard to the anchor point.

13.2   Dismount the trolley or trolley system. if it's a trolley system, the operational manual should establish the dismount process. First dismount the top trolley or the lower trolley is a decision of each

course and this will depend on factors like:
- the height of the lifelines
- the separation of the lifelines
- the type of pulley used

13.3   Once the trolley system is dismounted, the AG gives the participant instructions on the next step, which could be:
- head to an aerial bridge
- go to the waiting area
- go to the next zip line
- go to the photo taking area

13.4   One of the most important aspects is that the guide does not allow the customer to remain in the landing zone as the next participant landing could collide with and occur an accident.

13.5   Independently the landing protocol of each course, the landing area must be clear and secure before providing the signal to receive the next participant.

14. Retrieval Protocol

Sometimes it may happen that there are parts of Equipment alone in the zip lines. This Equipment can be in the zip line for several reasons:

14.1   Slipped out of the hand of AG the at the time of the installation.

14.2   A transfer-type rescue was performed, and the Trolley was left in the Zip Line.

When this situation happens, the AG must do a retrieval. If this equipment is not removed from the lifeline, there is a risk that the participant will collide with it and an accident can occur. Each course can have its retrieval process. in general terms, the retrieval process contains the following steps:

14.3 Mount a Prusik, connect it to the Guide Trolley system.

14.4 The guide zip until getting to the piece of equipment. This approach should be with caution. Arriving at high speed could cause a collapse of the guide with the piece of equipment.

14.5 When you get to the piece of equipment, active the Prusik to stop the movement, and you can disconnect the Equipment with both hands.

14.6 When disconnecting the equipment, connect it in your harness in the side loops.

14.7 Once ready, remove the Prusik and head back to the platform.

15. Belay

The term belay implies a security action. ACCT defines belay as an individual or group action to handle the tension of a lifeline, with the intent of protecting the user in the heights. Belay is a controversial and complex work because there are many variations. In practice, adventure activities are never completely safe, and belay adds an additional security measure.

In the Zip Lines/Canopy Tours when you use the word belay, its involve actions such as:

15.1 Use systems in case something fails.

15.2 Use systems to stop or control a person descending or ascending ropes and vertical climbs.

15.3 Descend an individual from a high element.

15.4 Connect a second lifeline to a person doing Rappelling in case something fails or loses control.

15.5 Control the rope of the person who is doing Rappelling.

15.6 Connect a rope to a climber in case it falls while climbing.

16. Types of Belay

In the Zip Lines/Canopy Tours you practically use two types of belay:

16.1 Static belay

16.2 Dynamic Belay

16.1 Static Belay

In static belay, the participant is connected to the anchor using a lanyard. In other words, the connection is between the harness and the anchor. This type ok Belay restricts the participant's movement and should not allow it to pass beyond the edges of the platform. For that reason, there is no need for fall arrest systems.

16.2 <u>Dynamic Belay</u>

In dynamic belay the rope is anchored to the participant's harness, passes through a top direction point (pulleys, carabiner, friction reducers) and goes to the ground, where a second person (belayer) controls the rope with a Belay device. The dynamic belay is a type of Top Rope. On the ground, the Belayer needs a belay device to control the rope.

Taking into consideration that there is a great variety to do Belay, then there are several ways in which Belay is generally used in Zip Line/Canopy Tours

17. Belay systems in the daily Course preparation

Each day the course closes its operations, the equipment associated with Belay is collected to be washed, maintained, inspected, documented, and stored. The next day, an AG will have the responsibility of access the high elements to be able to install the Belay systems, ropes, carabiners, slings, pulleys, and all the Equipment associated.

Since Belay systems are not installed at the time of the course opening, it is not acceptable that the AG climb free devoid of safety (without Belay). Accessing the unprotected high elements could be an emergency if the guide falls from the top. It is unacceptable that the AG climb the element without Belay, it is not a good risk management practice, because the AG doesn't have the benefit of that protection. This situation is known as Leading Edge Environment. This means provide safety to the guides while installing Belay systems in high elements.

In practice, in the Zip Line/Canopy Tour industry methods for the protection of the AG have been instituted. These are composed of anchor points, where the guide can be secured while installing the Belay systems. These practices should be performed by an experienced guide. Some of the techniques used to access the Elements without Belay are:

    17.1   Replace Belay's Rope

    17.2   Vertical Steel Cable

    17.3   LEAP-type anchor points

17.1 <u>Replace Belay's Rope</u>

At the time of dismounting Belay's rope, it is connected to the end to a utility rope. When you pull the belay rope, the utility goes into function, so you can remove the belay rope and leave the utility rope installed. At the time to install de belay rope, just connect the belay rope end to the utility cord that was previously installed. Also, this utility rope protects (belay) the guide during the belay systems' installation, because is used for climbing or ascending the rope.

17.2 Vertical Steel Cable

Another method to access the high elements is through a vertical steel cable climbing system. This type of system consists of a vertical steel cable parallel to the vertical structure where the Guide ascends or climb. This steel cable is anchored parallel to the ascent structure and permanently connected. To climb, the worker connects a steel cable blocker to the steel cable, which in turn is connected to a lanyard with an energy absorber to the Guide harness. If the Guide falls, is protected with a fall arrest system.

17.3 LEAP-type anchor points

The LEAP is a piece of steel that is screwed to the surface for providing an anchor point for the user. Then, when the course is endowed with these type of anchor points, the AG climb using a double lanyard or lobster claws, to access high element and install Belay system.

This method used must be executed by the most experienced guides. In addition, the processes to install the Belay systems must be documented in the Operations Manual, in order to be a standard procedure among all guides.

18. Elements Belay

As discussed above, there are several instances where the Guide must install and use Belay systems. Before describing the Belay techniques, the devices used to perform the task are presented.

18.1 Statics Belay

It is important to highlight the fact that static belay is composed of a single or double lanyard connected from the user's harness to an anchor point. In that case there is no movement, only a static or direct connection between the user and the anchor point. In the Adventure Courses static belay is used in the following activities:

    18.1.1 Connect in the zip lines

    18.1.2 To cross aerial bridges

    18.1.3 To cross horizontal elements

    18.1.4 To be connected to a belay cable while doing a course tour, or exceeding obstacle.

18.2 Dynamic Belay

In Zip Line Tours, the dynamic belay is associated with the horizontal and vertical elements, vertical climbing walls and the descent of participants from the platforms. In dynamic belay there is movement, that means that there must exist a device to control that movement and the friction of the rope.

The Dynamic Belay can be performed with:

18.2.1 Air Traffic controllers (ATC)

The ATC are pieces of equipment that are used to provide belay and to descend ropes. Some manufacturers manufacture them for both tasks. This piece varies and can be from a plate to a tubular piece, where one or two bights of the rope pass through a carabiner (connected to the harness) and come back out of the ATC, creating a rope curve that becomes sharper as friction is applied. One disadvantage is this, if the AG does not operate properly, the rope will run free through the ATC and cause an emergency.

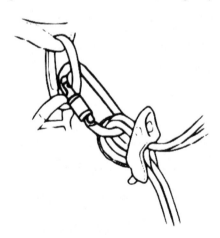

18.2.2 Automatic devices

The word automatic refers to the fact that the natural function or position of the device is to brake. That is, without Belayer action and if a fall occurs, the device will automatically arrest

it. To descend the user, it is necessary to use a handle that releases the rope and the person can descend. Its main characteristic is a clutch that assists in braking under a shock load.

18.2.3 Munter Hitch

Using friction knots, such as the Munter Hitch, to make belay the participants of the Adventure Tour, must be the last option. Handling the risks should be the first goal of the adventure program, for that reason, it is recommended to use automatic belay devices. The Munter Hitch is a last resort that in case of an emergency, allows the guide to make belay or descend a participant in a controlled way to the ground.

19. Anchors for Belay

Dynamic Belay systems are essentially 1-to-1 (one-to-one) ratio systems. That is the case when we make Top Rope and Belay participants from the ground, who are going to descend from a platform or are climbing vertical Elements. This means that the descending participant will transfer their weight to the Belayer on the ground, by balance effect, the Belayer will be lifted off the ground

To avoid this situation, when using Top Rope to descend individuals from platforms or some high Element, with Belayer on the ground, it must be connected to an anchor point on the ground. In this way, the sling anchored in the ground will avoid its lifting. The best recommendation is to anchor the descent device to the anchor sling on the ground. In this way, The Belayer will not feel pressure on the harness when descending to the participant and it will not be lifted.

19.1 How to connect the rope to the participant's harness?

To perform a dynamic belay, one end of the rope must be connected to the participant's harness. There practically 2 methods for connecting the belay rope to the harness of the participant:

19.1.1   Using Ropes with manufacturing terminations

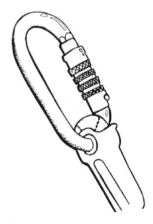

19.1.2   Use rope with knots-like Figure 8 on a bight, Double figure 8 or Bowline

91

20. Belay Systems

Within the wide variety of existing belay systems, the Zip Line/Canopy Tours uses 2 types. the AG can implement these systems in the different Elements according to the case and the necessity. Belay's systems types are:

20.1   Top Rope

20.2   Top Belay

20.1 Top Rope

ACCT defines the Top Rope as a belay system where the participant is protected by a belay rope that is determined or redirected above his/her head, and rope is taken out by a Belayer or belay beam. In other words, is a type of belay in which the participant is connected at the tip of a rope that passes freely through an anchor located at a higher point, and the rope goes down to the Belayer on the ground.

This type of belay is used on 3 occasions:

20.1.1   Descend participants from platforms.

20.1.2   Descend participants from the elements.

20.1.3   Protect vertical climbers.

In the Top Rope technique, it is recommended that the Belayer on the ground use an automatic belay device, because once installed, its block the rope automatically. By activating the handle, promotes the movement of the rope, the brake hand helps to support and control the friction and movement of the rope in general. All automatic devices require the brake hand to grip and control the rope.

20.2 Top Belay

Belay technique is used to protect the participant from high. For that reason, it is used when the AG are in the heights. This type of belay is used on 3 occasions:

20.2.2   Descend participants from the platforms.

20.2.3   Protect participant doing rappelling.

20.2.4   When the guide is on a platform or in a high element and need to descend a participant, the top belay can be used with the following devices.

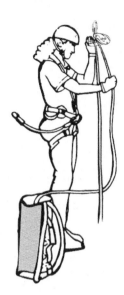

21. Belay devices to perform belay from the top

21.1 Belay from the top with Automatic devices

The next picture shows the correct way to install the automatic belay device from the top.

It is important to redirect the rope with a carabiner so that the rope runs correctly by the device.

21.2 Belay from the top with ATC

The next picture shows the correct way to install the ATC to make belay from the top. Make sure the ATC is designed to perform Belay from the top.

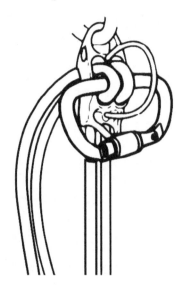

21.3 Belay from the top with Munter Hitch

The next image shows the right way to make Top belay using the Munter Hitch. Note that you need a redirection of the brake rope to improve the efficiency and friction.

22. Transfers

The transfer occurs when a participant changes or transfers from one Element to another. Because it cannot be devoid of protection at any time, it is not acceptable to disconnect the lanyard and then connect it to the new element. In these cases, it is necessary to use a double lanyard also known as Lobster Claws. When the lanyard is transferred from one anchor to another, the second line remains connected. That way, the participant will never be deprived of protection at the time of being changed or transferred from one element to another.

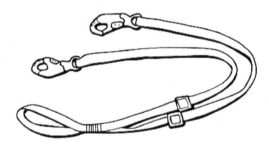

In courses that use static belay and, in effect, use the transfer process:

22.1   Transfer processes must occur under the supervision of an AG or the Course facilitator.

22.1   Before the participant enters the Course, make sure that the lanyard or the static belay sling is appropriate according to the height of the participant and the Elements to be performed.

22.2   In the heights the participant must be connected with at least one lanyard.

22.3   The AG needs to position itself where it can have a clear view of the participant's lanyard as well as the transfer process.

22.4   In courses where the transfer occurs at

20 feet or less, the AG can supervise from the ground. At more than that height, the AG should be in the Course with the participants.

23. Rappelling

Rappelling is the art of descending a lifeline at a controlled speed to avoid accidents. The individual who descends only has to control a total fraction of the weight of his body in order to control the descent.

Rappelling involves a series of techniques to descend using a rope in a controlled way. For the purpose of this Manual, only basic elements of Rappelling will be discussed. It is important to take in consideration that the Adventure Guide must use double rope. Using 2 ropes offers more alternatives at the time of descending a participant and at the moment of being the guide that descends.

23.1 Why Rappel is possible?

It is possible to rappel because the following occurs:

23.1.1   During descent, the friction created between the rope and the descent device determines the control.

23.1.2   The friction is created by the practitioner with a single movement of the rope in the opposite direction to the descent movement.

23.1.3   The movement may be controlled by the belay or the user.

23.1.4 The result of friction is heat produced by the kinetic energy.

23.1.5 The amount of heat produced depends on the height, the speed of descent and the weight of the practitioner.

23.1.6 The Belay device converts the kinetic energy into heat, which is then dispersed in the air in the form of noise.

23.2 Participants doing Rappelling

In some courses participants can Rappel, it means that they control their own descent device. In this case, the guide installs a Top Belay system, to protect the participant in case something fails or loses control. That way you use double rope.

23.3 Guides doing Rappelling

Most likely when the Guide do Rappelling will have no one to manage the top belay. It may be that another Guide is present, but, It's not always the case. This means that sometimes a Guide is alone at the descending platform. In this case, it is not acceptable that the guide uses a single rope. Remember, the rule is double rope at all times. In this scenario, the guide should use a Belay device that permits the use of double rope as a Figure 8 or a Rappel Rack. In case of using an automatic device, which allows only a single rope, the second rope is used for belay connecting an automatic blocker to the user's harness must be used. This way, if something fails, the user will be locked on the second rope automatically.

23. 4 The basic components of the Rappelling are as follows:

23.4.1 Anchor Point

23.4.2 Rope

23.4.3 Descent device

23.4.4 Harness

23.4.5 Belay

23.4.6 Personal Protection Equipment

23.4.7 Technique

23.4.8 Trial

24. Reasons to interrupt the Tour

There are reasons or situations that may require immediate termination of the Zip Line Canopy Tour operations. Closing may occur for the following reasons:

24.1 Climate

24.2 Emergency situations

24.3 Catastrophes or fatalities

24.4 Collapse of an element

24.5 Interruption of communications

24.6 Labor situations with the AG

It is important that these reasons are documented in the Operations Manual and all the guide knows them. Once one of those situations are presented, guides have to know when to close the operation for the safety of the clients and the staff.

Unit 8
After the Tour

There are aspects related to risk management and the work and responsibilities of the AG at the end of the tour. In general, once culminate the adventure, the AG performs the following tasks:

1. Check-Out process

During the Checkout process, the participants return the PPE and other Equipment that was provided to them and/or rented. That's the time to return back the backpacks, cameras, helmets, harnesses and others. At this time, it is important that the AG verify that the Equipment was recovered complete and with all its components. At the same time, he must make an inventory to make sure got back all the Equipment used. In addition, at these stage customers can complete some documents, pay, complete a report, etc.

2. Equipment Management

Once the equipment was picked up, the risk management practices lead the AG to wash and disinfect them.

Once clean, put them to dry and store it in the designated place. It is important that the AG check the Equipment, which has not been returned with any damage or malfunction that may affect the participation of other customers. If defective equipment is found damaged or missing components after the tour, the course must have a document to report and discard the affected equipment. After these processes, the equipment must be ready and stored for the next tour or take it out to discard for maintenance.

3. Completing Documents

After making the tour, the AG must basically complete some standard documents such as Tour Log, which documents everything that happened during the tour. Other documents may be for specific situations such as an incident report or accident report. As mentioned above, there must also be documents to report the damage and other situations with the equipment. On the other hand, if during the Tour, the AG noticed some situation in the structures of the Course that need inspection or maintenance, document and reports it and send it to the person in charge.

The Operations Manual must establish which are the documents and for which situations they must be used.

4. Inspections & Maintenances

If during a Tour there are situations that need to be inspected or maintained, those must be addressed before the next day or the next Tour. It is a basic risk management practice to document and address all situations that may affect participants. Therefore, if an AG finds a situation during the operation, they must be documented and served by the staff in charge.

5. Transportation

If customers are picked up for transportation on a bus, it is important for the AG to

accompany them and make sure that occurs in a safe environment. Customers may have an accident or incident in the transportation. The AG must make sure all their customers are on the right bus, depending on the hotel, cruise, or excursion. In addition, you must ensure that all completed the processes, documents required, delivered all the Equipment and have all your belongings before you leave.

6. Preparations for the next Tour

At the end of the tour, and perform each one of the necessary tasks, it is important that the AG ask themselves, Did I make all the preparations for the next tour? If the answer is no, you automatically must go to complete the processes. If the answer is yes. will be ready for next group or adventure day.

Unit 9
Technical Rescue

Sometimes equipment fails, a pulley with flaws means that it will not move, so a guide will have to go to the rescue. The rescues in zip line have a special connotation. Treatments, while someone is suspended from a lifeline in a harness, are practically impossible. Opening the airways and giving CPR is impossible because of the cervical consequences it could have. It is important to recognize if harness syndrome is present.

In this case, the priority is to make a rescue maneuver either to descend or move the participant to the nearest platform. Once the participant is safe outside the zip line system, provide first aid and/or follow the emergency plan. A chest harness to stabilize the participant either because they are unconscious or overweight, is an excellent piece of equipment that must be taken in the rescue bag.

On some occasions and for different reasons, it is necessary to execute rescues in the zip lines. Some reasons may be:
1. Malfunction of the pulley
2. The participant loses consciousness
3. The pulley is derailed

In these and other possible situations it is necessary to get closer to the participant and perform a rescue. Remember the harness syndrome. The participant cannot be left hanging a long time without movement.

1. What is a Rescue?

A rescue is a location, access, stabilization, and transportation to a safe place or to health care a person at risk. In the adventure course, a rescue involves all the actions that run from communicating a security information to helping an individual physically when he is in a dangerous situation. Being on the heights and in dangerous places with the risk of fall, need to use of ropes techniques and specialized Equipment to be able to handle them. Guides who act as rescuers need the skills to execute that kind of task.

2. Operational Rescue Protocols

Operational Rescue Protocols (ORP) it's a label to group a series of steps, actions and considerations before executing a rescue. At the time of the technical rescue, it is not acceptable for the AG simply to zip without any specialized Equipment, as well as without any consideration, analysis, or assessment of the situation.

For that reason, no matter what type of rescue it is necessary to execute, either in a zip line, descending participants from the platforms or descending ropes, always and by basic protocol, it will be necessary to make certain steps before connecting a rope or zip to rescue a client in trouble. Because each Course and each situation and conditions are different, some steps may not apply in certain cases. The steps or stages of the ORP are the following:

3. Rescuer's attitude, leadership, and behavior

Rescues in the heights either in zip lines or descending a rope, are of high risk and dangerous. It is essential that the AG be properly trained and certified to execute this type of procedure.

A guide without the necessary knowledge and experience could aggravate the situation. Technical rescues need maneuvers, rope techniques that sometimes require specialized equipment or use the same equipment, but with other purposes. Situations like harness syndrome may complicate things if they are not answered immediately. For these many other reasons, the AG that works as a rescuer must be a leader and possess the correct competencies

4. Harness Syndrome

When an individual hang from the harness without movement, the slings tighten and create a kind of tourniquet that constrain the circulation of blood vessels in the legs, pressing the arteries, and obstructing the blood circulation and that creates heart problems.

Long hanging periods may result in extreme pain, blood buildup in the legs, and changes in blood pressure. This situation creates a possible fatal condition that increases as the time passes. The consequences are unconsciousness and possible death in minutes. In some cases, up to 10 minutes.

When the harness acts as a tourniquet, it is not advisable to remove it immediately when lower that person to the ground and removing the harness. Cases have been reported where the accumulated acid blood, by releasing the Tourniquet (harness), runs from a blow to the heart and other organs, which could result in the failure of a vital organ, including the heart.

An action that the rescuer can perform to alleviate the headgear syndrome and its consequences is to elevate the legs and loosen the straps on the legs of the harness. If the participant is aware, the guide can instruct him to move and elevate their legs as high as possible. Also, the guide can help the participant by elevating their legs and placing them on the rescuer's legs. Another method that the guide can use is to use an Etrier to keep his legs elevated. With these three actions, you can stimulate the blood circulation through the body.

Having comfortable harnesses, with wide cushioned slings, can help to hang up longer before physical and psychological problems occur. Of course, the biggest recommendation is to provide immediate help to any individual who for some reason is hanging without movement in his harness.

5. Approaching the injured

Approaching the injured is the process of approaching a participant in trouble. At the time of a rescue, the AG (the one who is sending and the one who is receiving) must ask themselves which of the two will be responsible for executing the rescue in the zip line. This answer must be reflected in the emergency plan.

In practice, both guides should be able to perform the rescue. Why? Because the decision of which one will execute the rescue must be based on where the participant is positioned, not which guide possesses more experience.

As a rule, the zip line is divided into two areas. The first area starts from the take-off platform to the lower part of the lifeline. The second area is from the lower part of the lifeline, to the landing platform or the ascent.

If the participant is positioning at any point in the descent, even at the bottom, the best recommendation is that the rescuer comes from the top side in relation to the participant, that is, the Guide on the take-off platform. The purpose is to avoid a collision with the participant, in case the brake fails and continue zipping.

In other case, if the participant passes the lower part of the zip line and/or is at some point of the ascent, then the guide on the landing platform must perform the rescue. In this case, because the participant passes the lower part of the zip line, he could move towards the guide for deflection and normally that does not generate high speeds, so it reduces the probability of a collision.

If only one of the guides owns the equipment and is qualified, he/she must carry out the rescue from any direction and take all the considerations and precautions necessary to avoid a collision or other situations while approaching the participant.

5.1 To approach the participant, the Guide must perform the following steps:

5.1.1 The AG must be connected on the platform using a lanyard.

5.1.2 Tie a Prusik knot in the upper cable (if the system is double) or in the main lifeline. A further consideration could be tie the Prusik in the lifeline which does not possess a brake block, to avoid an obstacle in the traverse.

5.1.3 Tie a Prusik knot in the direction of the platform and connect the other end of the cordage in the larger vertebra of the carabiner below the Prusik knot. In other words, in a double cable system, the cordage connects to the carabiner linking the pulleys, if the Prusik is tied on the top line. On the other hand, if the Prusik is connected to the bottom lifeline, the other end of the cordage must be connected to the larger axis of the carabiner in the lower pulley.

5.1.4 In the case of approaching from the landing platform, if the brake block is extended, this could be an obstacle to approach the injured. In that case it is necessary that the rescuer bring back the brake block to the platform to clear the lifeline in order to be able to approach the participant.

5.1.5 Disconnect the safety lanyard before going to the rescue.

5.1.6 The AG should cross the zip line with one hand in front of the pulley and the other behind the Prusik Knot. The hand in front of the pulley is for controls the speed of his movement and with the hand behind the Prusik pushes it to slide, avoiding a stop in the zip line. Depending on the zip line angle of inclination, and the location where the participant stopped, it will be the speed and control that the guide will have to manage.

5.1.7   When the guide approaches the participant, he must release the Prusik knot to block and stop the rescuer's movement, leaving it in the correct position to exert. The next step is to connect the participant.

5.2 Connect to Participant

Connecting the participant refers to the action of connecting a lanyard between the rescuer and the participant. With this action, the participant is prevented from continuing the movement and positioning away from the rescuer. The purpose is to have both, rescuer and participant together during the rescue. When approaching an injured customer, the first action of the rescuer should be:

5.2.1   Connect the participant lanyard to the rescuer trolley system. The participant lanyard must not be connected to the rescuer's harness. In case of a failure where the participant falls, all the weight goes down to the rescuer harness causing undue force and

pressure. The lanyard of the participant must be connected in a trolley system, either the rescuer or a new one.

5.2.2   If the participant does not have a lanyard, the rescuer must have an extra one to connect it from the participant harness, to the rescuer Trolley system or a new Trolley system.

5.2.3   In the specific case of the Norwegian Reeve rescue type, the rescuer lanyard must be connected after the participant trolley system. The participant trolley system, must be between the rescuer and his lanyard.

6. Using the Chest Harness in Rescues

In rescue situations, the chest harness is sometimes necessary. Therefore, the AG needs to know and identify situations when it is necessary to use it. In what type of case the chest harness may be necessary:

6.1 Zip Lines

Trolley Transfer: the participant chest harness is connected should be connected to his trolley system using an accessory cord. The accessory cord can be connected to the chest harness with a Girth Hitch or a basket.

6.2 Rappelling

Descents from platforms or zip lines: using an accessory cord the participant chest harness of is connected to the lifeline, above the knot that connect the participant. The accessory cord can be connected in the chest harness with a Girth Hitch or a basket.

7. Anchor Point Selection

Sometimes the rescue may be based on descending a client either from a platform or from a zip line. In this case, is essential an anchor point to connect the descent device or the belay system:

Some considerations for choosing the anchor point:

7.1 Connect an anchor manufactured for those purposes.

7.2 Use yoke zip line anchor, as an anchor point.

7.3 Use eye bolt zip line anchor, an anchor point.

7.4 Use anchor strap, as an anchor point.

7.5 For the purpose of lower down participant from the platform, use the trolley system connected to the zip lines. The guide must have the experience to decide if that is the best alternative to descend an individual and what anchor point y the properly to use.

8. Rope Rescue

In some rescues the use of ropes is indispensable. The fact of being in a zip line and being elevated in platforms, requires that the ropes are well coiled and organized to be ready the time of being required. The best recommendation is to keep the ropes in specialized rope bags for this. That way, you can travers the zip lines or handle the ropes from the platforms in a better organized way, do not occupy space, and greatly reduce the possibility of entanglement.

8.1 The ropes are used in the following rescues:

a. Descending individuals from the zip lines.

b. Descending individuals from platforms with top belay, bottom belay, or stop rope.

8.2 Commands to manage the rope:

a. Guide: "Clear for rope"

b. Bottom Belayer: "Clear"

c. Guide: "Rope"

9. Client Check

The client check is a security protocol that the AG performs before transferring a participant to a new anchor or belay system. The purpose of this protocol is to ensure that everything is correctly installed before the rescue process is performed.

9.1 The Client Check consists of the following steps:

9.1.1 Participant

9.1.2 Anchor Point

9.1.3 Belay System

9.1.4 Rope

9.1.1 Participant

In this stage the Guide verifies that all the PPE of the participant is properly fitted. Check helmet, harness, lanyard, trolley system…

9.1.2 Anchor Point

Check that everything is connected correctly in the anchor point either you use a yoke, Eye bolt, anchor strap or Trolley system.

In addition, check:

a. Knots

b. Carabiners

c. Anchor components and parts are in positions and all connections are verified.

d. Other anchor components

9.1.3 Belay System

Check all parts of belay system. Belay's system may be:

a. Bottom Belay

b. Top Belay

c. Top Rope

9.1.4 Rope

In reference to the ropes, before executing the rescue maneuvers, the AG must verify the following:

a. The rope is properly stowed in the bundle without tangles.
b. The rope is bent correctly in the rope bag.
c. Rope is free of knots, tangles, and kinks.

10. Rescues

Next, description of various types of basic rescues used in Zip Line/Canopy Tour:

10.1 <u>The Monkey Style</u> - this type of rescue is used to tow the participant with its own Trolley System to the nearest platform.

10.2 <u>Mechanical Advantage</u> – This type of rescue is used to pull the participant towards the platform, dividing its total weight to pull less weight to the most efficient rescue.

10.3 <u>Trolley Transfer</u> – This type of rescue is done when the participant's Trolley System fails, and its movement stops. With this rescue, the participant is transferred to the rescuer Trolley or to a new one, to take the participant to the platform.

10.4 <u>Norwegian Reeves</u> – This type of rescue is done when the participant's trolley system fails, and its movement stops. With this rescue, the participant is transferred to a lifeline or belay system to be descended to the ground or transferred to the rescuer Trolley system.

10.5 <u>Lowering from Platform</u> – With this type of rescue the participants are descended to the ground from a platform.

10.6 <u>Pick-Off</u> – This type of rescue is executed when a participant is stopped while Rappel down. In this case, the participant is transferred from his rope and descent device to the rescuer's rope and descent device.

The Monkey Style

This type of rescue is used to tow the participant with its own trolley system to the nearest platform.

Steps

1. Do the command "not to send", in case that the rescue is executed by the guide of the landing platform.

2. Instruct the customer to stop, so that progression is not continued. This command could be verbal or manual.

3. Performs the Operational Rescue Protocol (ORP).

4. Connect the Participant.

5. The guide should turn on his back and push himself hand after hand heading towards the platform. The Prusik should be loose enough so that it can slide in front of the rescuer's pulley and at the same time sufficiently adjusted so if the rescuer stops, the Prusik stops him in the same position.

6. Once they reach the platform, the first step is to connect the rescuer lanyard in the anchor point to prevent them from coming back again.

Mechanical Advantage

This type of rescue is used to pull the participant towards the platform, dividing its total weight to pull less weight to the most efficient rescue.

1. Do the command "not to send", in case that the rescue is executed by the Guide of the landing platform.

2. Instruct the customer to stop, so that progression is not continued, This command could be verbal or manual.

3. Performs the Operational Rescue Protocol (ORP).

4. Before going to the participant, have a rope with a termination that can be connected to the participant's harness, like a figure 8 on a bight knot.

5. Connect the Participant – In this type of rescue, the lanyard of the participant is not used, it remains at the same connection point. In this case, the rescue rope is connected to the participant harness. That's the rope that will be used for the mechanical advantage later. Is important to keep the rope in a rope bag to have more control and do not tangle with the system.

6. Before returning to the platform, if you have the concern that when the participant returns, continue the trajectory and move away from the rescuer, keep the participant in position with a Prusik connected from the zip line to the participant Trolley system.

7. Once the guide reaches the platform, the first step is to connect his lanyard in the anchor point to prevent coming back again.

8. Connect the mechanical advantage System 3:1 in the anchor point.

9. Connect the 3:1 system with the rope previously connected to the participant and performs the mechanical advantage until it reaches the platform.

10. The first step when the participant arrives is to connect his lanyard to an appropriate anchor point.

Norwegian Reeves

One of the techniques to rescue participants in zip lines are known as Norwegian Reeves. Through this technique, the guide can transfer from trolley to trolley, or lower down a participant to the ground. This rescue should be used if the pulley stops and is not able to continue traversing the zip line.

With the Norwegian Reeves Technique, two methods of rescues can be used; Transfer the participant from trolley to trolley or descend the participant to the ground from the zip line. Specifically, the technique of transferring from Trolley to Trolley can be executed with the help of the participant. In case that the participant is unconscious, another type of method that can be used and describe in this section.

1. **Assisted Trolley Transfer**

    Techniques used to transfer the participant to another Trolley system with the help of the participant.

    - Method Using an additional Trolley System.
    - Method using Rescuer Trolley System.

2. **Non-Assisted Trolley Transfer**

    Techniques used to transfer the participant to another Trolley system without the help of the participant.

    - Method using an additional Trolley System
    - Method using the rescuer Trolley System

3. **Lower Down the Participant**

    Technique used for transferring the participant to the belay system to control the descent to the ground.

Assisted Trolley Transfer
Method Using an additional Trolley System

Steps

1. Do the command "not to send", in case that the rescue is executed by the guide of the landing platform.

2. Instruct the customer to stop, so that progression is not continued. This command could be verbal or manual.

3. Performs Operational Rescue Protocol

4. Connect the participant

5. Mounts an additional trolley system between the rescuer's trolley system and the participant's trolley system. Make sure that the additional trolley system is connected some point in the rescuer harness, if the trolley system falls out of his hands, the trolley system should stay connected to the rescuer's harness. Once the additional trolley system is ready, connect it to the participant harness.

6. Connect an Etrier in the upper zip line, between the new Trolley system and the rescuer.

7. Arrange the Etrier on the participant's feet and hands on this or in the zip line, as appropriate.

8. Ask the participant to stand, to release the tension of his affected trolley system and dismount it.

9. Once the affected trolley system is dismounted, the participant will be connected in the new trolley system.

10. After that, if the client is able to continue by himself, can make a monkey movement to return to the platform.

11. If the participant does not have the capacity to move by itself, the AG must perform a monkey style rescue to assist the participant to the platform.

12. Once they reach the platform, the first step that the rescuer must execute is to connect his lanyard to the anchor point to prevent them from returning back.

Assisted Trolley Transfer
Method using Rescuer Trolley System

Steps

1. Do the command "not to send", in case that the rescue is executed by the Guide of the landing platform.

2. Instruct the customer to stop, so that progression is not continued. This command could be verbal or manual.

3. Performs Operational Rescue Protocol (ORP).

4. Connect the participant.

5. Connect a Etrier in the upper zip line between the rescuer's Trolley system and the participant's Trolley system.

6. Arrange the Etrier on the participant's feet and hands on zip line.

7. Ask the participant to stand, to release the tension of his affected trolley system.

8. When releasing the tension, disconnect the trolley system lanyard that is connected to the lower pulley and connect it in the rescuer trolley system.

9. When the participant returns to position, he will be connected to the rescuer Trolley system.

10. Disconnect participant trolley system.

11. After that, the guide has to continue the zip line traverse doing the Rescue Monkey Style to return to the platform.

12. Once they reach the platform, the first step that the rescuer must execute is to connect his lanyard in an anchor point to prevent them from returning back.

Non-Assisted Trolley Transfer
Method using an additional Trolley System

Steps

1. Do the command "not to send", in case that the rescue is executed by the Guide of the landing platform.

2. Instruct the customer to stop, so that progression is not continued. This command could be verbal or manual.

3. Performs Operational Rescue Protocol (ORP).

4. Connect the participant.

5. Mounts an additional trolley system between the rescuer and the participant. make sure that the additional trolley system is connected some point in the rescuer harness. If the trolley system falls out of his hands, the trolley stay connected.

6. Once the additional trolley system is mounted, connect it in the participant harness.

7. Connect the 4:1 to the participant harness.

8. Connect the 4:1 to the participant harness.

9. Once the mechanical advantage system is connected, pull the rope to lift the customer. If necessary, use a Jumar type hand ascender to pull the rope from the mechanical advantage system. At the same time, the Jumar serves as a "stop" so that the load (the participant) stays elevated once it is lifted because the Jumar gets stock with the 4:1 pulley. Some 4:1 systems have an integrated cam that when pulling the rope the raised weight is automatically locked and keeping it raised. Continue lifting until the participant's Trolley system is loose enough and without tension to be able to be disconnected from the participant's harness.

10. Once the participant is lifted, disconnecting the affected participant's trolley system, and returning it to its normal position, after removing the mechanical advantage system, the participant will be connected to the new trolley system.

11. Connected the participant to the rescuer trolley system, do the Monkey Rescue Style and move to the platform.

12. Once they reach the platform, the first step that the rescuer must execute is to connect the safety cap at the anchor point to prevent them from returning.

Non-Assisted Trolley Transfer
Technique using the rescuer TS

Steps

1. Do the command "not to send", in case that the rescue is executed by the Guide of the landing platform.

2. Instruct the customer to stop, so that progression is not continued. This command could be verbal or manual.

3. Performs Operational Rescue Protocol (ORP).

4. Connect the participant.

5. Connect a 4:1 Mechanical Advantage System (Piggy bag), in the lower pulley of the rescuer Trolley system or in the lifeline.

6. Connect the 4:1 to the participant's harness.

7. Once the mechanical advantage system is connected, pull the rope to lift the customer. If necessary, use a Jumar type hand ascender to pull the rope from the mechanical advantage system. At the same time, the Jumar serves as a "stop" so that the load (the participant) stays elevated once it is lifted because the Jumar gets stock with the 4:1 pulley. Some 4:1 systems have an integrated cam that when pulling the rope the raised weight is automatically locked and keeping it raised. Continue lifting until the participant's Trolley system is loose enough and without tension to be able to be disconnected from the participant's harness.

8. With the participant Trolley system become loose, disconnect it, and connect it in to the rescuer Trolley system (lower carabiner).

9. Dismount the participant's affected trolley system from the zip lines.

10. Releases the mechanical advantage system and allows the participant's weight to fall into the rescuer's trolley system.

11. Once with the participant in the rescuer's trolley system, he must assume the position of the monkey and move towards the platform.

12. Once they reach the platform, the first step that the rescuer must execute is to connect his/her lanyard in the anchor point to prevent them from returning back.

Lower Down the Participant

Technique used for transferring the participant to belay rope system to control the participant's descent to the ground.

Steps

1. Do the command "not to send", in case that the rescue is executed by the guide on the landing platform.
2. Instruct the customer to stop, so that progression is not continued. This command could be verbal or manual.
3. Performs Operational Rescue Protocol (ORP).
4. Connect the participant.
5. Connect the belay device in the lifeline (in steel wire cable has to use steel carabiner)

6. Connect a 4:1 Mechanical advantage system (Piggy bag), in the lifeline. Connect it in the lower pulley of the rescuer Trolley system or in the lifeline, just depend on the case

7. Once the mechanical advantage system is connected, pull the rope to lift the customer. If necessary, use a Jumar type hand ascender to pull the rope from the mechanical advantage system. At the same time, the Jumar serves as a "stop" so that the load (the participant) stays elevated once it is lifted because the Jumar gets stock with the 4:1 pulley. Some 4:1 systems have an integrated cam that when pulling the rope the raised weight is automatically locked and keeping it raised. Continue lifting until the participant's Trolley system is loose enough and without tension to be able to be disconnected from the participant's harness.

8. Connected the rescue rope with the belay device to the participant's harness.

9. Disconnect the participant trolley system.

10. Once you have disconnected the participant Trolley system, release the 4:1 tension so that the individual goes down and held by the rescue rope. At that point remove the 4:1 and connect it in the rescuer harness.

11. Now the injured one is on the rescue rope, ready for descent.

12. Remember, the Belay device must be locked in position while the 4:1 is being dismounted, to be sure that the participant will not descend uncontrollably at any time.

13. Ready, descends the participant with control using the belay devices.

14. For this method it is recommended to use automatic belay devices. This offer more control and safety during the rescue process in general.

15. If you are using another type of device such as Figure 8 or a Rappel Rack, be sure to have them with the safety knot at the time of transfer to the participant.

Lower Down from Platforms

Sometimes problems occur with our clients that prevent them from continuing the tour. It could happen when the participant is located heights in a platform and there is no possibility of descending. There are no stairs or other structures that allow the participant to go down back to the ground. In this type of situation, it is necessary to carry out a rescue that consists of lowering down the participant to the ground.

One things to notice is if the person is conscious and can assume the position in a harness. Otherwise, the person will have to be lowered on a rescue stretcher with a rope system.

When performing this technique to lower individuals, it is important not to connect the belay device directly to the rescuer harness. The weight of the person will cause pain to the rescuer and affect his harness by weight in different directions. This can result in physical damage and/or pain to the rescuer, including harness rupture. When a person is descending from heights, the belay devices is connected at an anchor point and the rope in the person harness. In this way, the person's weight is directed directly to the belay device and to the anchor point, not to the rescuer.

Lower down participants from the platforms

There are two basic methods that the AG can use to descend individuals from the platforms:

1. Top Rope
2. Top Belay

Lower Down participant with Top Belay

1. The participant, as well as the rescuer must be connected with their respective lanyards to an anchor points on the platform.

2. Connect Belay's device to the anchorage point and install some redundancy. The anchor point can be a Trolley system installed on the double or single lifeline, located at the edge of the platform. The belay device is connected to this Trolley system. It is important that the Trolley has a sling anchor from the main anchor point to restrict the Trolley to the desired position.

3. Install the rope on the Belay device. The rope must be contained in a rope bag to keep it organized and tangle free. The Belay device recommended is the automatic.

4. It is important to follow the manufacturer's recommendations when belay devices are used for top belay. In some cases, is necessary install a carabiner superior to the belay device to redirect the rope for friction and function purposes.

5. Perform a client check before connecting and descending the participant with the belay rope.

Client Check

Anchor check

Belay Device Check

Rope Check

6. Connect the rope to the participant's harness and position him at the edge of the platform.

7. Before beginning to descent, disconnect the participant's lanyard. Start to descend and control the participant to the ground using the belay device.

8. Provide the necessary instructions before the participant descends.

9. It is important that the rescuer remains connected to his lanyard at all times during the rescue.

10. If you are using another non-automatic belay device, such as a Figure 8 or a Rappel Rack, it is important to know how to use these devices for top belay. If necessary, in these types of devices the brake rope can be redirected with a carabiner to the main anchorage or other point. That way the AG will have better control of the belay device.

Lower Down participant with Top Rope

1. The participant and the rescuer must be connected with their respective lanyards to an anchor point on the platform.

2. Connect the top rope with redundancy. The anchor point can be a trolley system installed on the double or single cable, located at the edge of the platform. The top rope is connected to this trolley system (Figure 8). It is important that the Trolley has a lanyard connected from the main anchor to restrict the trolley to the desired position.

3. Install the Top Rope using of figure 8 that is recommended for this case.

4. Perform a client check before connecting and descending the participant with the belay rope.

5. Connect the rope to the participant harness connection point and tuck on the edge to descend.

6. The other side of the rope should be thrown down to the ground and controlled by the AG that will perform the belay from the ground.

7. Provide the necessary instructions before he descends.

8. Disconnects the participant lanyard of the and the descent begins.

9. Before start to descent, make the right command to make sure that the Belayer on the ground is ready to perform the task.

10. Start communicating with the belayer on the ground while the descent is made so that this is controlled form.

11. It is importance that the rescuer on the upper platform is connected to his lanyard during the rescue. The AG doing the bottom belay has to be connected to another lanyard to the ground to prevent that the 1:1 effect from lifting the ground and losing control of the descent.

Pick off

In some adventure courses, part of the activities that are realized is "Rappelling". In this activity, the participant descends a rope on a vertical wall controlling his own descent. In courses the rappelling can be in:

1. Natural walls (cliffs, waterfalls, canyons, mountains, rocks).

2. Artificial walls (climbing walls, buildings, structured bridges).

3. High elements.

4. Aerial platforms.

5. Adventure towers.

6. Aerial bridges.

During a descent, a situation may occur when the participant is stopped on the rope without movement. After applying the rescue protocol, the AG has to Rappel down to provide assistance. The AG can assist the person to descend or transfer the participant to the AG system to release him from his descent device. That technique is known as "Pick off." Then, the purpose of this type of rescue is to descend to the participant, transfer him/her to the system of the rescuer, and descend it in a safe and controlled way to the ground.

During a rescue of this type, the anchors, ropes, and other equipment are subject to increments in weights by loads that come in different directions. For that reason, several factors need to be taken into consideration:

5. Anchors must be multi-directional.

6. Carabiners must be properly closed, aligned, and monitored for proper position.

7. Ropes, lanyards and other Equipment must comply with the safety factor 10:1.

8. The AG should be prepared for extra weight, so it needs to use more friction during the rappel down.

Pick-Off Strap

The Pick-Off strap is an adjustable flat webbing that is used to connect the rescuer to the participant. This type of strap is used to make rescues in rappelling situations. This strap is versatile for connecting the participant, adjusting it and then lowering it connected to the rescuer's descent device.

Steps to follow to perform the Pick Off techniques

1. Before the rescuer descends to the participant, he/her must connect the pick off lanyard to their descent device. Connect the other end (the adjustable one) in a place that does not confuse or interfere.

2. Make sure rappel down with a rescue device manufactured for two people.

3. Descend to the participant, stop and secure the descent device. It also assures that of the participant, if necessary.

4. If the victim is suspended in the rope, the rescuer must stop with his legs at the hip level of the participant. The rescuer can use his legs to stabilize him. In this maneuver, the rescuer must be a little higher than the participant.

5. Connect the adjustable side of the rescue sling (pick-off) to the participant harness. If the lanyard is a fixed size, make sure it is not a very long or short distance that makes the rescue impossible your connection and rescue. If the sling is with buckle, it in the injured and adjust until it is as close as possible to the rescuer.

6. Once the pick-off strap is connected, activates participant descent device so that the weight is transferred in its entirety to the rescuer's descent device. At this time the AG should maintain the classic descent position by positioning the participant between his legs.

7. Once ready, the rescuer must control the participant descent until it reaches the ground.

Unit 10
Incidents & Emergencies

The Zip Line/Canopy Tour are high-risk attractions where an emergency could occur at any time, without being anticipated or expected. The ACCT standard recommends that the course has an emergency plan that establishes and at the same time prepares an organized answer all the adventure guides (AG) and other staff at the course. Each adventure program must have its own emergency plan adjusted to the conditions, location and resources and location of each course. This section will be presented in a general way, which are the steps to follow if an incident or emergency occurs.

1. Incidents

An incident is an unplanned minor event that does not result in any injury or damage but has the potential to do so. This situation involves risk management measures to prevent them from reoccurring later. When incidents occur, they must be reported and documented. That is a legal defense because the participant, later, could make a claim.

The incidents must be reported.

The incident report safeguards the responsibility of the AG as it is the only evidence of the response that was made during the incident. So, the incident report is a risk management measure that details what happened and what was the response treatments.

Some of the situations that can be considered incidents and must be reported:

1.1 Any staff member gave first aid.

1.2 Required attention beyond a normal case.

1.3 Requires follow-up in the field by the AG.

1.4 Requires follow-up of a doctor.

1.5 Requires follow-up on the part of a Therapist, social worker, psychologist, etc.

1.6 It requires the use of medicines.

1.7 Interferes with the active participation of the individual.

1.8 Requires evacuation or rescue from the field or adventure activity.

1.9 The situation has the potential to provoke an insurance claim or a customer's legal claim.

1.10 The situation involves motor vehicles.

1.11 It requires to take the participant out of the tour for reasons of behavior, motivational, psychological or medical.

1.12 Requires the use of communication radios in the field.

1.13 It involves the violation of the Local Operation Procedures (LOP) or the local laws.

2. Stress

During a real rescue situation, the body's shoot hormones, transform the person, wave the heart of the AG, fear invades and, as a result, we experience what is known as the tunnel vision. That is, when we look through a tubular structure we can only look to the front and lose perspective what happens on both sides and even more what happens behind our backs. The real goal is to follow the PE and use the skills learned, for what you were trained.

3. Emergency Plan

An Emergency Plan (EP) is a document that has a series of procedures designed to direct an organized response in the event of an accident. A vital component of the EP is that it establishes the guidelines and procedures for managing emergencies. The key components of an emergency plan are:

  3.1 Access to the situation

  3.2 Provide the initial response

  3.3 Manage the group of participants

  3.4 Contact the emergency service

  3.5 Medical

  3.6 To transport the handicapped to the hospital institutions

  3.7 Notify Employee Team

  3.8 Inform the relatives of the injured

  3.9 Inform the media.

4. Emergency Response

When it is imminent to perform a rescue operation, it is time for the AG to concentrate, follow the EP, make the right decisions and, above all, remain calm and in control. The AG must begin a series of coherent steps in order not only to rescue the participant, but also to ensure their own safety, and the safety of other AG and the rest of the customers.

Rescuers are individuals also susceptible to environmental conditions, wounds, illnesses, exhaustion and emotional changes. Consequently, they could become victims. All AG must be able to follow the EP at the time that occurs. Taking into consideration that each course possesses its plan, it should have the following parts:

Step 1: Activate the Emergency Plan

When a situation occurs, the first step is to activate EP. At that time, all AG and other staff must know its role and position within the plan. That's not the time to practice or improvise. By activating the emergency plan, the AG must execute for what was trained.

Step 2: Access

Once the plan is activated, the next step is to approach the participant. At this stage, it is important to ensure the safety of the rescuers. If there is a person harmed, it is inconceivable that by a mistake they become two victims. Therefore, the AG should perform a quick but effective evaluation to the scene. Until the AG determines that the scene is safe for itself, it should not approach the affected person.

For example, if a participant is lying on the ground because he was hit by a dry branch that fell from a tree, and the AG is not noticing and stops right next to it, there is a likelihood that it will also be impacted by another piece of branch.

In this same way, flooding, rocks falls, thunderstorms, wild animal attacks, a participant unconsciousness in high platform or element, and many other situations can be dangerous for the rescuer AG, so they must be evaluated before entering the zone of the emergency.

Step 3: Stabilization

Once the guide is convinced that the scene is safe for him/her, the attention must be directed to the stabilization of the victim. This is a very important and sensitive procedure. An individual who has suffered a fall, accident or illness may be conscious or unconscious, face up or face down, including hanging on the rope or a zip line. The first step is to check the state of consciousness.

If the victim answers you, try to get information about what happened and its medical condition. In case of being on the ground, the AG must be able to evaluate the injured and start with the first aid processes. In case of being on a rope or in a zip line, the AG must maneuver to lower down the affected person to the ground as quickly as possible.

Step 4: First Aid

In an emergency where it is necessary to apply first aid, the program need a trained AG. Participants can face a series of physical and/or emotional traumas

that will need help. Even the guides must be prepared to provide CPR. In the emergency plan, this position is critical and there should always be an AG ready to assume it.

Step 5: Emotional stabilization

First aid is not just blood and broken bones because of a collision in the zip lines, but also involves emotional aspects. A frightened and nervous victim is a potential danger to the rescuers and to itself. Talking to the victim is the best way to reassure her. Invite (a) to breathe deep, to tell what happened or to talk about another subject if necessary to distract their attention. Solidarity with him/her, let him know that he is not alone and that you are prepared to help him to the last consequences.

Step 6: Rope rescue

As discussed in the rescue protocol, go to execute a technical rescue, with ropes and other pieces of Equipment to make systems, must be the last alternative.

Before that, the AG must evaluate the first three steps of the protocol. No doubt there are times where the AG must go right ahead to the rope rescue. So, the emergency plan must provide for an AG to always cover that position.

5. The Adventure Guide and the Emergency Plan

5.1 Each Guide should know his or her position and tasks at the time an accident occurs, and the plan is activated.

5.2 The guide should be able to weigh which is the best response according to the Emergency Plan.

5.3 The AG must be able to make decisions.

5.4 The AG must be trained to follow the rescue protocol, jumping on the rope or the zip line is not the first answer.

5.5 The AG must have rescue equipment according to possible situations that might occur.

6. Communication during the emergency

Caution should be exercised when is time to communicate during an emergency. The adrenaline and the stress of the moment, can make it leak insider information, which customers and other participants should not know. A comment, lack of respect, or something sensitive being heard by a client or participant, can be the difference between success or in a legal situation. Some of the issues to be considered about the communication are as follows:

6.1 Use the radio channel reserved for emergency situations.

6.2 It is important to confirm to be sure that the partner heard clearly what is said, either personally, through radio or cell phones.

6.3 Pay special attention to words that may resemble, pronounce in the same way, or have double meanings.

6.4 Call people by their first or last name to make sure the message gets to the right person.

6.5 Communicate your decisions or change decisions to another AG, do not assume that they will know.

6.6 Communicate dangerous situations when you detect them, do not assume that the other AG will know.

6.7 Not communicating any type of medical information such as diagnosis, cause of accident or other sensitive information.

6.8 Communicate the necessary resources or Equipment in a clear way.

6.9 Keep in contact with the professional emergency response, answer their questions and report what has happened.

7. Leadership during an Emergency

Undoubtedly, professional emergency management have developed authoritarian positions to structure and manage rescues. In Zip Lie Tour the traditional positions take a special connotation because the emergency will be resolved by Adventure Guides. Therefore, the training of the Guides and their roles during an emergency, must be clearly set out in the plan. There are at least 3 basic positions that the Emergency Plan must have written in detail:

7.1 Person in charge of the rescue

7.2 First Aid

7.3 Rescuer

7.4 Ground support

7.1 Person in charge of the rescue (Incident Commander)

Probably this position is occupied by the owner, or the operator of the course or the most experienced AG. That person will be the leader of the coordination, execution and emergency management.

7.2 First Aid (first responder)

This position should be occupied by the AG with more experience and/or certifications in the subject of first aid and emergency. The ACCT standard recommends that at least one person be certificated for these purposes. The responsibility for this position is to provide medical assistance to the injured.

7.3 Rescuer

This position should be occupied by the AG with more experience and/or certifications in the subject of rope rescue and/or zip lines and emergency managements. The responsibility of this position is to install the technical systems either to descend by ropes or go in the zip line and execute the technical rescue. This person must be well experienced and certified for those purposes.

7.4 Ground support

This position may be occupied by employees of the company trained in the Emergencies Plan. Basic tasks for this position:

7.4.1 Incident Command

7.4.2 Support for medical staff

7.4.3 Support for rescue personnel

7.4.4 Manage equipment

7.4.5 Provide First Aid & CPR

7.4.6 Prevent and inform any existing hazards

7.4.7 Manage customers and visitors

7.4.8 Communicating with the emergency medical and/or emergency management system

7.4.9 Protect victims and/or injured

7.4.10 Help manage internal communication.

8. Documentation

At the end of the emergency or incident situation, it is of paramount importance to document the event. This document could be:

8.1 Incident Report

8.2 Accident (SOAP) Report

8.3 Tour Log

Unit 11
Training Tool

A basic knowledge of teaching and learning before designing a training for the Adventure Course staff is essential. According to Noe (2005), training is the effort planned by a company to make it easier for its employees to learn job-related skills. These competences are divided into three categories:

    1) Attitudes

    2) Skills

    3) Knowledge

According to ACCT (2016) a successful training provides the opportunity for practitioners to develop knowledge, skills and understanding, in order to provide effective and consistent experiences to the participants. When designing learning, these categories should be taken into account as they will help to define the training module related to specific competences. The question would be, who establishes the skills you need, and the guides of the Zip Line Tours? First, the powers are established in the laws of zip lines or adventure in the countries they own. Labor or recreational laws may establish requirements. In countries that do not have industry specific laws, the recommendations with the greatest validity worldwide are those of ACCT. ACCT recommends the general and specific competences that Adventure Guides and other Adventure Course facilitators should possess.

On the other hand, there is the work of the person in charge of the training or the instructor. The work of this is double because it has to identify the basic skills for the performance of a job but also to provide training programs that promote advanced learning related to the goals and strategic objectives of the Adventure Course. Many companies have adopted this broader perspective in training, which includes the concepts of high leveraging and continuous learning (Noe, p.4).

1. Training Program

Part of the operation of the adventure course is to have a training program whose purpose is to train the Adventure Guides among other employees. The ACCT standard requires that the instructor be a qualified person. That has an implication for the Owner / Operator since, to comply with the standard, you need to locate a qualified person in charge of the training program. In addition, training based on ACCT standards, must be offered in adventure courses certified by inspectors or PVT of ACCT.

The training program is composed of two parts: The training provided by the company itself or those of the home, and certified professional training offered by third parties or other professional companies. The ACCT standard provides for both situations.

2. Professional Training

The employee in charge of the Training Program is given the task of looking for a company or a qualified person to offer the training. In case of being certified courses, the ACCT standard establishes that it must be offered by a "Certify Body" which is the organization in charge of issuing the certificate in turn, this organization has to comply with a series of standards to be able to provide certificates.

The person in charge of the Training Program is responsible for coordinating at least once a year or more frequently if necessary, training with professional companies. The Course must ensure that the instructor they hire meets the expectations. One recommendation is to ask for recommendation letters, ask for references or see them giving courses to other Adventure Courses.

3. Internal Training

The In-House Training Program must have a qualified individual to offer the training. Internal trainings have to be offered at least once a year, but, the more frequent, the AG will perform better. It is important that the training plan considers the competencies that AG need and that therefore is designed based on those criteria. On page # an example of a training plan is offered.

4. Below, a series of recommendations to consider when designing training or training for the AG that meet the ACCT standards are presented:

4.1 The training must be documented and offered in a course certified under the ACCT standards. This certification is issued by a professional inspector certified by ACCT or by a PVM.

4.2 The content of the training must comply with the operating standards of ANSI / ACCT 03-2016.

4.3 The training or training must be designed based on the technical competencies proposed by ACCT to operate the Course effectively.

4.4 The inspector must provide a specific manual of the topics that will be worked on by each of the participants.

4.5 Internal training must be offered at least once a year. The best recommendation is to make them as often as possible. The more the AG are trained in the required competences, the better their performance in the Adventure Course.

4.6 The training includes high risk activities, for that reason it is important that the instructor handle the risks during the trainings. Furthermore, when they are new AG, apprentices, they do not know the Teams or the associated risks. In addition, it must provide reasonable accommodations for people with disabilities.

5. Training of Adventure Guides

Once the Instructor selects the competences that he wants to instruct, he will be ready to create his training plan. In other words, as it will instruct AG, what strategies, methods and educational activities will be used to ensure that the training develops knowledge, skills, and understanding. Below is the following information that can be used by the instructor to develop his Training Plan:

5.1 Seven Steps in the Instruction Design Process

5.1.1 Carrying out a needs assessment. Are there gaps in employee performance? Do the employees have the attitudes, skills, and knowledge necessary to meet the strategic goals and objectives?

5.1.2 Ensure the preparation of employees for training. Do employees possess the necessary motivation and pre-requisite skills?

5.1.3 Create an appropriate learning environment. Are the learning objectives and instructional materials meaningful to the student's learning?

Is the physical environment well organized and conducive to learning? Do employees receive supportive feedback?

5.1.4 Ensure the transfer of learning. How will learning affect the real world?

5.1.5 Develop an evaluation plan. What are the expected results? How will you measure the results of the training?

5.1.6 Select the training methods. Do training methods include opportunities for students to apply new information and techniques related to real-life problems in the workplace? Online? Face to face? Hybrid?

5.1.7 Evaluation of the training. Do employees benefit from the training? Did the training result in both learning and transfer of learning? What were the costs of the training compared to the benefits?

These steps allow the trainer to ensure that the training experience is meaningful, relevant and meets the current needs of the competency gaps of the Course employees. Based on the needs assessment, the personnel carrying out the training can gather information about the training needs of an organization. It is about analyzing the A (attitudes), S (skills) and K (knowledge) of the members of the organization and identify performance gaps between the "real state" of ASK and a "desired state".

The training can then be designed to close the gaps. According to Noe (2005), competencies are areas of personal skills that allow employees to successfully perform their jobs by achieving results or performing tasks (p.95) As mentioned above, ACCT provides a series of necessary skills for the operation of the Zip Line Tour. In addition, there are specific aspects in each Course, each one needs specific skills to operate. The preparation of the training is done in a systematic way and allows the organization to address all these specific aspects.

Once the design process is completed, that is, from determining the specific needs to the evaluation of the training, then proceed to the next step. The next step is to take each of the identified needs and create training modules directed to each need. Pike (2003) explains the eight grounds for the proper preparation of these modules.

6. Eight (8) steps for proper preparation

Step 1. List of your needs. Assess needs in at least two different ways (for example, survey, interview)

Step 2. Evaluate your audience
Determine the current level of experience and knowledge of the participants (Do not underestimate or overestimate what practitioners know).

Step 3. Decide your goal: Develop instructional objectives. How do you do this? Identify attitudes, skills and / or knowledge that participants will acquire as a result of their training.

Step 4. Plan your approach. How will you introduce the matter?
Start with a hook to engage the public. Make it fun.

Step 5. Develop your lesson.
State clearly the objectives, the progression of the lesson and the evaluation. More information on how to create a lesson plan later in this chapter.

Step 6. Plan the application of your lesson.

Step 7. Plan a transfer activity.

Step 8. Collect materials; Prepare the room (If the class is live.).

6.1 Some considerations when following the preparation steps:

Create a table that lists the instructional objectives, the focus and material needed to deliver the lesson or module.

Instructional Objectives	Focus	Materials

This table illustrates the macro components of the training. Each module must have a lesson plan. There are many lesson plan schemes. A simple, but effective lesson plan is listed below:

Title: The title of the lesson

Objectives: The knowledge, skills and / or attitudes that participants are expected to learn

Materials: Audiovisual Equipment, visuals, among others.

Delivery method or description: Steps to follow to offer the lesson.

Evaluation and / or Assessment: The type of measurement to be able to ensure that the objectives of the lesson were met.

There are several learning theories that guide the facilitator of the training. This book discusses one of these theories that has proved useful in the training of professionals in the field of recreation and outdoor education. This theory is **The nine events of instruction of Gagne.**

7. Learning theories

Learning the theories helps to understand the perspective of the training and allows the coach to create a plan that is effective. Let's start with Gagne's theory.

8. The Nine Events of Instruction of Gagne

The nine instructional events of Gagne are a form of psychological education, Robert Gagne. The steps take into account and address the mental conditions necessary for learning, observed by Gagne, and can be adopted in your own classroom.

The nine events are the following:

8.1 Get attention

Get the attention of the class because they will be involved in an activity and / or discussion (Use breaks ice, games, stories, etc.).

8.2 Inform Goals

Let the class know what the learning objectives are so they will be able to organize their thoughts around the lesson (Describe the learning activities)

8.3 Stimulate the recovery of the previous Learning.

Develop prior learning so that students can take advantage of previous knowledge or skills (teach previous lessons, relate information to previous topics, include activities where previous knowledge is used)

8.4 Present the Content

Present the content of the learning through lectures, activities, discussions, exercises and other methods of instruction.

8.5 Provide Guidance

Give students enough guidance during their learning (provide specific information on activities, expectation reports, and delivery times).

8.6 Obtain Performance and Practice

Allow students to apply knowledge and skills learned (use activities, group work and individual)

8.7 Provide Feedback

Give constructive feedback to the students by highlighting one thing they are doing well and one thing they can work on a little more.

8.8 Evaluate Performance

Student performance evaluations allow them to see where they are exceeding and where they need more practice.

8.9 Improve Retention

Allow students to apply personal connections and increase retention by personalizing information (allowing opportunities for students to relate their learning to activities with previous experiences).

At the time of applying this theory to training, the facilitator can use practical tools to carry it out. Two practical tools are the 3D's and IDEAS acronyms.

9. 3D's & IDEAS Models

These two models to be used in the teaching-learning process bring to light the theoretical framework of Gagne. In turn, when they are used effectively they contribute to the understanding, accommodation and application of concepts, skills and behaviors (attitudes).

9.1 3D's Model

DDD = Demonstrate, Do, Debrief

9.1.1 Demonstrate skills to your audience.

9.1.2 Have your audience do / practice the skills they learned.

9.1.3 Discuss the components of practice and skills to ensure understanding.

9.2 IDEAS Model

9.2.1 **Introduce** the topic with a question or a small piece of information about the importance of the skill you are about to learn

9.2.2 **Demonstrate** the skill

9.2.3 **Explain** the skill step by step

9.2.4 **Activity**, where they practice the skill

9.2.5 **Summary** of the 2 main points and

The use of creativity in the development of training programs is not limited to the creation of lessons or models for teaching. The use of visuals, toys and / or Equipment contributes to the effectiveness of the training. Below is a list of accessory tips and tools to carry out the training of the adventure guides.

10. Tips and Tricks for teaching the training:

Use accessories

10.1 Sketch for scenarios or medical practices.

10.2 Ropes, pulleys, harnesses for demonstrations of their use.

10.3 Small pieces of rope for simulations and practices of knots.

10.4 Index cards and post notes for group discussions.

10.5 A shower curtain with concepts to be used as a visual aid (instead of a blackboard or PowerPoint).

11. Instructor tools

11.1 Bring a waterproof notebook to take notes on the performance of the participants.

11.2 Tablet with camera to record the team during practices or simulations.

11.3 Use applications such as Google Form or Poll Everywhere to evaluate learning.

11.4 Use Case Studies

11.5 Create the scenario or practice previously to ensure that it is aligned with the objectives of the lesson or module.

11.6 Understanding the outdoor classroom: What are the basic needs of the participants?

11.7 Expose your audience six times to an idea, with interval reinforcement to increase knowledge retention to more than 90% (Pike, 2003).

11.8 When setting up the outdoor classroom, think about where the sun is or will be for the training and position yourself in front of it, so that the participants do not have to squint. If possible, bring camping chairs and a flipchart for flexibility in chair arrangements.

11.9 Create pre-made posters with some of the contents or visual aids for training. This helps with time management and activates visual learners.

11.10 If your outdoor classroom allows you to tape the visual aids and posters to the wall or trees or set up a line of fabric.

Repetition and exposure to these visual aids.

11.11 As mentioned earlier in this chapter, in the Seven Steps in the Instructional Design Process, the evaluation of the training is the final step. The evaluation should identify the benefit of training for employees and the organization. In addition, you must measure the impact on the operation and the programs. After each training each participant must be evaluated in four levels. The four levels are:

11.11.1 Reaction

11.11.2 Learning

11.11.3 Behavior

11.11.4 Results

12. Evaluation Techniques

Each lesson must have an evaluative aspect. The acquisition and retention of knowledge must be measured immediately and 60 days later. There are several evaluation techniques.

The techniques below have proven to be effective in the outdoor recreation and education industry:

12.1 Observation of skills and abilities

12.2 Demonstration of skills and abilities

12.3 Rubric with specific criteria

12.4 Video recording of the employee performing the necessary tasks

13. Continuous training

Training is a continuous event, not a day or a week. One should think about the quarterly training, continuous training with mentors, quarterly meetings, online training, among others. It is important to remember that training begins with the employee hiring process and assimilation to the workplace. The ACCT standard requires at least one training per year. Possibly it is very little compared to all the skills and knowledge that the Adventure Guides need to do a professional task.

Authors

Dr. Luis D. Acevedo

Luis was born and raised in Cupey Bajo, Puerto Rico. At 10 years of age his mother, Milagros Rivera, took him to a Boys Scout meeting and that changed his life; he devoted himself to outdoor education and adventure. Acevedo holds a Master's degree in Environmental Sciences and a Doctoral Degree in Education. Luis has over 25 years of experience working with Adventure Courses and Educational Programs based on Adventure. He is a Professional Inspector certified by the Association for Challenge Course Technology (ACCT). He is a professor at the University of Puerto Rico. He currently resides in San Juan, Puerto Rico. He travels the world doing course inspections and staff training to promote safety and the highest quality of programing. Email: airelibrepr@gmail.com

Dr. José H. González

José was born and raised in Puerto Rico. He started his professional career in outdoor education in the 90's working for major organizations including Hurricane Island Outward Bound School, Thompson Island Outward Bound Center, Dartmouth College Outdoor Programs, Plymouth State University and NOLS Wilderness Medicine. Currently, he teaches at California State University Northridge, shaping the next generation of outdoor recreation leaders. José has been an active member of the Association for Challenge Course Technology (ACCT) for the last decade. He holds a Doctoral Degree in Education with a focus on Curriculum and Instruction. Jose lives in San Diego with his wife and two young sons.
Email: josegonzalezsanders@gmail.com

Made in the USA
Las Vegas, NV
08 May 2022

4836663R00090